Praise for Lee Duncan and
Double your business

'In two years, Lee helped me to double my turnover, motivate my staff, and work half the hours I used to.'

Chella Heyes, owner of Zoom Answer Call, Cambridge

'With Lee's guidance and a lot of hard work, I grew my sales by 148% in just 11 months.'

John Carmichael, owner of Superwarm Services Ltd, Edinburgh

'If you want cotton wool then Lee is not for you. If you are looking for an honest, to the point, solution-focused business expert then Lee is your man.'

Nathan Siekierski, Managing Director of Jasper's Franchise Ltd

Double your business

How to break through the barriers to higher growth, turnover and profit

Lee Duncan

PEARSON

Harlow, England • London • New York • Boston • San Francisco • Toronto • Sydney
Auckland • Singapore • Hong Kong • Tokyo • Seoul • Taipei • New Delhi
Cape Town • São Paulo • Mexico City • Madrid • Amsterdam • Munich • Paris • Milan

PEARSON EDUCATION LIMITED

Edinburgh Gate
Harlow CM20 2JE
Tel: +44 (0)1279 623623
Fax: +44 (0)1279 431059
Website: www.pearson.com/uk

First published in Great Britain in 2012

Pearson Education is not responsible for the content of third-party internet sites.

ISBN: 978-0-273-75949-2

British Library Cataloguing-in-Publication Data
A catalogue record for this book is available from the British Library.

Library of Congress Cataloging-in-Publication Data
Duncan, Lee.
   Double your business : how to break through the barriers to higher growth,
turnover, and profit / Lee Duncan. -- 1st ed.
      p. cm.
   Includes index.
   ISBN 978-0-273-75949-2 (pbk.)
   1. Small business--Management. 2. Marketing--Management. 3. Consumer
satisfaction. I. Title.
      HD62.7.D856 2012
      658.02'2--dc23
                              2012002677

10 9 8 7 6 5 4 3 2 1
16 15 14 13 12

Typeset in 9/13pt ITC Stone Serif by 3
Printed and bound in Great Britain by Ashford Colour Press Ltd, Gosport, Hampshire

For Julie, Michael and Rachael – I know how much you have sacrificed to allow me to write this book. Thank you.

In memory of my father, Ronald Edward Duncan.

Contents

About the author

Lee Duncan is one of the UK's leading business growth coaches. Working with ambitious small and medium businesses, both in the UK and internationally, Lee has helped his clients achieve a staggering £40 million of extra business.

Lee's family tree has its roots firmly in enterprise, dating right back to the early 1800s. He grew up surrounded by small family businesses and this clearly showed in his behaviour at school, where he was nicknamed 'Duncan Enterprises'.

After almost two decades in increasingly senior positions in the corporate world, Lee set his entrepreneurial spirit free when he switched to full-time business coaching. Lee has since been engaged by some 200 businesses and his influence extends further, to the many thousands who have heard him speak or read his publications.

Despite his obvious intelligence (he holds a first class Honours degree), Lee has a very direct, no nonsense style and has been described as 'the most plain-speaking and effective consultant you will ever meet'. This style is mirrored in his writing; you will find very little jargon and no complex theoretical models in this book, just practical and immediately applicable advice.

For relaxation, Lee can be found tinkering with computers or making hardwood furniture.

Acknowledgements

When, in March 2010, Paul Simister called me to put together a virtual mastermind group, it set the ball rolling for this book. Through Paul I met the wonderful Sonja Jefferson, whose dedication to connecting authors and publishers resulted in a call from Pearson, so, to both of you, I am deeply grateful.

When I stalled as I was writing the book, Ian Brodie, Heather Townsend and Jonathan Senior gave me the shove I needed to get going again – I appreciate you being cruel to be kind!

While Liz Gooster made the initial moves regarding the book, she left Elie Williams to experience the whooshing sound of deadlines racing past – something I now know is the daily worry of every editor. Thanks Elie, for your trust and flexibility, letting me work the way I do best – under pressure!

The preparation of a book for publishing is a bigger task than I anticipated. For helping me to produce the book I have always wanted to write, I owe a debt of gratitude to my Australian editor extraordinaire, Robert Watson. Your fanatical attention to detail and 100 per cent commitment were instrumental in making this book what it is today. I shall miss our early morning and late night conversations.

This book could not have happened without the confidence that so many clients and colleagues have placed in me over the years. I cannot possibly name all of you, but special mentions must be made of a few. I'd like to specifically name Paul Marsden, Bahi Sivalingam, John Carmichael, Trevor Nicholls, Chella Heyes, Ian Selby, Darren Pescod, Carolyn Mumby, Terry Ruddy, Tim Gale, James Neal, Graham Abbey, Rod Wilson, Trevor Nicholls, Andrew

Rowbotham, Mark Newey, André Goodison, Ben Lee, Jamal Shahid, Mohammad Akram, David Lewsley, Toni Hunter, Paula Wigg, Dr Steven Aronson, Philip Mashinchi, Jonathan Bell, Alan and Nina Dicks, Richard Pakey and Nathan Siekierski.

Sincere thanks also to Dr Paddi Lund for giving me unique insights into customer service that I could never have learnt from a book. I hope we get the chance to do it again sometime.

Introduction

Success in business requires training and discipline and
hard work. But if you're not frightened by these things, the
opportunities are just as great today as they ever were.

David Rockefeller

Many books about growing a business describe it as a
series of simple steps, as simple as baking a cake. If
it were that easy, every small business would become
a flourishing enterprise. Although, of course, there are those
people who, with some talent and luck, seem to sail effortlessly
through from start-up to multimillion-pound empire, in reality,
most people struggle after getting their business going.

So, when the publisher approached me to write *Double your
business*, I was both thrilled and apprehensive, because I wanted
to write a book for the normal business owners, not just the
talented and lucky ones. That is where the challenge really lies,
because there are lots of reasons for businesses becoming stuck
or failing to grow. Each business that achieves success follows its
own path, navigating its unique set of circumstances to get there.
This book will help you to choose the best path for your business
and move quickly along it.

Before going any further, perhaps it would be useful to know a
little about my credentials for writing a book like this. At sixth-
form college, my economics teacher nicknamed me Duncan
Enterprises because of my ability to broker deals on everything
from high-end hi-fi to printed stationery. After a successful
corporate career, culminating in running a £28 million business
unit for a large corporation, I trained to become a business coach.

For the last decade, through my coaching practice and speaking engagements, I have affected the success of over 3000 businesses with practical growth tactics. Many have achieved growth of 100 per cent or more, with the most successful achieving 500 per cent growth.

Nothing is more important to my work than the success of my clients. I love the excitement that comes from taking a business that has been stuck at £500,000 turnover for a couple of years (or longer) and helping it to break through to £1 million and beyond within a year or two. This is not just a job for me, it is my passion.

The strategies presented in *Double Your Business* really can provide massive growth – I have seen it again and again. From time to time, a very small business will approach me for a kick-start to get them moving. One such recent case involved a small removals firm owned by two brothers. They had seen sales dry up and, despite trying everything they knew, it just wasn't working for them. During only three hours of consultations, we rebuilt their marketing, sales and quotations process, helping them to double their sales volume within a month. That is just as satisfying as helping a multimillion-pound travel firm to double its sales in less than two years, adding millions to its turnover in the middle of a recession that saw many of its competitors go out of business.

The idea of doubling your business is a simple one. Doubling isn't an outlandish aim; it is achievable in the space of one or two years. To sell twice as much, to earn twice as much profit and take home twice as much pay all have a wonderfully symmetric appeal to them. It does not have the seemingly impossible stretch of a tenfold increase. Of course, once your business doubles, the momentum to grow is established and so doubling again becomes the next target. The more I work with businesses, the more I am convinced that all good businesses can achieve remarkable growth quickly ... if they know what to do.

UK government statistics show that only 1 in 1000 new companies will achieve annual revenues of £1 million, while over 50 per cent don't survive past their fifth year. Business is clearly hard, but for those who are willing to commit their actions and thoughts to the task, the rewards more than make up for it.

Sometimes people in business think that working harder is the secret to success – putting in longer hours, doing more and more work. If, however, all you are doing is sticking to the same methods you've used for years, but working a bit harder, you will rarely produce growth (though it almost always helps to prevent a company slipping backwards). So, if you have found yourself working harder and longer without any noticeable growth, you need to take a step back and ask if you are mistaking *activity* for *progress*.

The real secret to success is not simply hard work – it is smart work. For example, it's fairly easy to add up your daily sales with a calculator every afternoon, but are you learning anything from that piece of work? How much more insight could you get by learning to use a software package that can highlight who is making the most sales, who your most profitable customers are, what marketing is producing the most new business, etc. Thinking outside the box and putting new ideas into action is what will get your business moving faster. That is what this book aims to give you – the smart tools to upgrade your thinking about business to give you a step change towards greater success.

Learning new tricks and putting them in to practice is not always easy, but it is the way to transform your business. The decision to be made is whether or not you are willing to pay the price for success. That price is not paid in cash, but in getting out of your comfort zone, learning new ideas, taking some risks and 'putting your back into it', as my Dad would have said. The results, my clients tell me, are well worth the effort.

How to use this book

This book is designed around the concept of Barriers to Growth. These are the reasons for a business generally growing for a while, then reaching a plateau and stubbornly refusing to grow any further. Where the problem is not market-related (it rarely is),

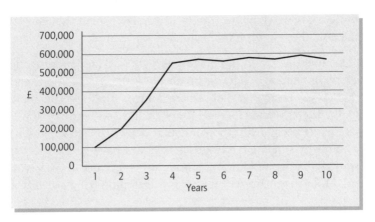

Figure 1   Typical performance of a business over time

the business is said to have hit a Barrier to Growth, which must be investigated and addressed before further growth will occur.

In Figure 1, this phenomenon is shown as it would appear if the annual revenues were drawn as a graph. For the first 4 years of the business, it grew at a rapid rate before it seemed to get stuck, at just under £600,000, for the next 6 years. This pattern – of growth followed by a prolonged plateau – is a symptom the business has hit a Barrier to Growth.

In this book, you'll find a diagnostic tool to help you identify such barriers and appropriate sections of the book will help you overcome them and kick start your growth. There is a total of 22 Growth Blueprints, grouped into the major business topic areas, to help you do just this.

Chapter 1 Break through your Barriers to Growth

This chapter explains the concept of Barriers to Growth and how the Growth Blueprints are used to overcome them. I've developed a simple questionnaire so that you can diagnose the problems affecting your business and go straight to the specific Growth Blueprints to deal with them.

Chapters 2–8 Growth Blueprints and Breakthrough Action Plans

Each of Chapters 2–8 provides a practical overview of a major business topic. The chapters are then structured as follows:

- **Introduction** to the topic, explaining why it is important to growth, and an overview of the two to five Growth Blueprints and matching Breakthrough Action Plans.

- **Growth Blueprint(s)** – these describe in detail how to break through each Barrier to Growth, with examples from real businesses and practical tips designed to offer thought-starters for you to apply in your business.

- **Breakthrough Action Plans** – these set out a series of action steps for readers to follow so you can apply the Growth Blueprint(s) yourself.

The Growth Blueprints are grouped into topics because many of them link together like jigsaw pieces.

In broad terms, the topics covered in each chapter are as follows.

- **Chapter 2 Growth blueprints to cultivate habits of success** how to develop the personal habits for success

- **Chapter 3 Growth blueprints for financial management** how to understand the basic financial information required to steer a business in the direction of growth

- **Chapter 4 Growth blueprints for leadership, management and teamworking** how to get consistently high performance from employees

- **Chapter 5 Growth blueprints for massive lead generation** how to generate leads and turn them into sales opportunities

- **Chapter 6 Growth blueprints for sales and sales management** how to sell more effectively and make the most of sales opportunities through effective management of salespeople

- **Chapter 7 Growth blueprints to stabilise, systemise and optimise your business** how to use procedures and systems to eliminate daily firefighting and allow the business owner to concentrate on growth rather than operations
- **Chapter 8 Growth blueprints for outstanding customer service** how to increase loyalty and generate customer referrals through outstanding customer service
- **Chapter 9 Case studies** examples of businesses that have overcome Barriers to Growth and achieved remarkable success through working with the author, using the Blueprints presented here.

Two other ways to use this book

While the book has been designed to be used as a way to find and address specific problems directly using the diagnosis question-naire in Chapter 1 and the individual Growth Blueprints, many readers will prefer to read the book from beginning to end in the conventional way. This will provide insights into all areas of successful small business management. The third way is to browse the Contents page and choose individual chapters to work on.

Finally ...

You can buy a book about advertising to increase the number of leads you generate. You can buy a book on customer service to improve customer retention. You can buy a book with clever ideas for upselling and cross-selling to lift sales. This book, however, does all three (and more) so that your whole business grows to unimaginable levels. The secret is to work through it, one Growth Blueprint at a time, until you, too, have doubled your business.

To have the chance to help thousands of businesses through the pages of this book is a privilege and a responsibility I was proud to accept. Please join up at www.double-your-business.com to access your free bonus items (including templates from the book), which will help you double your business and to make some new friends.

I encourage you to share your business success stories and any good anecdotes along the way – I may even include them in the next edition of this book, if you are happy to put yourself and your business name into print, of course. Running a business can be a lonely affair and having the chance to share successes with others who know what you have been through is satisfying in itself. I will also publish the best stories on www.double-your-business.com to share with other readers.

You can reach me via e-mail at lee@double-your-business.com

FREE* CD : Unlock your growth potential

Sales and marketing mastery with the Growth Blueprints

Lee has recorded an hour-long special CD for readers of *Double your business*. While any Barrier to Growth can hold a business back, ineffective sales and marketing are the top two issues for over 80 per cent of small businesses.

Great marketing and sales are the fuel for your growth and this CD explains how to generate results immediately from the sales and marketing-related Growth Blueprints, while developing them into a full-blown marketing and sales machine to power the growth of your business.

To claim your copy, visit www.double-your-business.com/CD and one will be despatched to you immediately.

Please note there is a nominal charge to cover postage and packing.

Disclaimer

This book is a guide to business growth. It should not be construed as offering professional business advice or considered a sensible substitute for such advice. If your business has problems, get some direct help with it rather than trusting to luck.

Break through your Barriers to Growth

A questionnaire to identify what prevents your business from growing

Clarity affords focus.

Thomas Leonard

While discussing the challenges of business with their owners, something became very obvious: every business reaches a plateau caused by a set of circumstances that require changes to be made. The changes may be to the way the team is managed, or marketing may need to be beefed up to produce more leads, or perhaps the business model needs to be reviewed to make it more profitable. The reasons that businesses hit plateaus are the Barriers to Growth.

There was once a boy who longed to fly away and experience great adventures. Early one cold morning, as he crossed a field of mist, he heard a tremendous roar. Looking up he saw the most magnificent hot air balloon floating just above his head. A ladder dropped down beside him and he enthusiastically clambered up into the basket.

He was met by an old man who had flown the balloon from deepest south to furthest north. 'Please', beseeched the boy, 'teach me to fly'. The old man said, 'Well, how do you think it works?' The boy looked around and saw a gold cord hanging down under the balloon. Eagerly he pulled the cord and, as the burners roared, heating the air inside the balloon, it started to float upwards. Giddy with delight, he tugged again to make the balloon fly higher, when, all of a sudden, it jerked to a halt. The boy tugged harder and harder still, until the balloon's burners were roaring with the effort and the balloon was so full its material came close to ripping.

No matter how hard the boy tugged at the rope and how loudly the burners roared their fiery heat, the balloon refused to rise any further. The old man said, 'You look to the sky and try to force the balloon to fly, but, when you only look upwards and pull that cord, you are deaf and blind to what is going on around and below you. Use your eyes and ears and you will discover what holds you down.'

The boy released the cord and looked over the side of the basket below the balloon. Hidden in the mists below was a strong rope tethering them to the ground. When he released the rope, the balloon began to rise again into the blue sky, towards a world of new adventures.

Your business is just like the balloon in this story. No matter how hard you try to drive growth, if you do not cut the ropes that hold you back, your revenues and profits will not move. The goal of this chapter is extraordinarily simple: to identify what is holding your business back and point you to the right place to fix it. If you can identify this limiting Barrier to Growth and deal with it, your business will rise to the next level. Overcoming one Barrier at a time is sufficient to give you better growth than you currently have. Tackling just one Barrier at a time also prevents overload and confusion!

It is common for a single set of changes to release a business to grow by as much as 10 to 30 per cent, with some businesses enjoying a doubling of their sales and profit after addressing a single one.

About the questionnaire

There are 22 Barriers to Growth presented in this book – drawn from the most common issues experienced in the businesses I have worked with. These businesses have doubled and added millions of pounds by addressing their Barriers to Growth. One business with revenues in excess of £25 million per annum failed when it did not accept a diagnosis and continued to work blindly on other areas (it was very busy, but making desperately low profit margins).

The Barriers to Growth are arranged in order of the impact they typically have on a business. So, for example, if the business owner is personally low in motivation (Barrier 1: Lost your mojo?), it is pointless trying to address marketing issues, because, without passion and enthusiasm, the business owner is unlikely to make anything happen.

Instructions

On the following pages, I have numbered and named each Barrier to Growth. Following each are four statements with tickboxes for you to mark if the statement is true for you and your business. This questionnaire will help you to identify your Barriers to Growth.

For many businesses, it will be a case of working through the list of Growth Blueprints, from 1 to 22, while others will simply need to pick their way through the list, addressing the areas as they are highlighted by the ticks in the boxes.

Go to the Growth Blueprint named below the questions in the chapter indicated. Read the entire chapter to gain a complete context for the work given in the Growth Blueprint, but take action only for the specific Growth Blueprint identified by the statement(s) you ticked.

When you have implemented the actions for that Growth Blueprint, return to the questionnaire and start again. In this way, you will address the key issues for your business and not have to take action where it would not be of direct benefit to future growth in your situation.

> **Success tip**
>
> In one case, a potential client with a £200,000 per annum business that would not grow told me his marketing and sales were excellent. Yet, my assessment was that these were precisely the areas that were not working.
>
> In a self-diagnostic test like this, you have nothing to gain by cheating!

Identify your Barriers to Growth

Barrier 1: Lost your mojo?

Your get up and go has deserted you.

- ☐ You feel burnt out and no longer self-motivated.
- ☐ Often you wonder why you bother with this business.
- ☐ Friends say that you look very tired or unhealthy and you don't have any bounce in your step.
- ☐ You are not very busy and you can't be bothered to get busier.

If you ticked two or more of the above statements, you need Growth Blueprint 1: Get your mojo back! (Chapter 2).

Barrier 2: Disorganised and lack focus?

Although you are busy, you struggle to finish things that would drive your business forwards.

- ☐ You are bursting with ideas and you want to run with all of them.

☐ There is so much to do that you don't know where to start.

☐ You are bogged down and don't get important tasks done because you forget them.

☐ You wish you were far more organised and efficient than you are.

If you ticked two or more of the above, you need Growth Blueprint 2: Get organised and focused (Chapter 2).

Barrier 3: Cash flow problems?

Your business is active and busy, but the bank account seems to stay empty.

☐ Your business spends more than it makes.

☐ Customers are very slow to pay or there are bad debtors who will never pay.

☐ Money is tied up in slow-moving or dead stock.

☐ There are insufficient funds to complete your work-in-progress.

If you ticked one or more of the above, or otherwise know you have cash flow issues, you need Growth Blueprint 4: Properly managed cash flow (Chapter 3).

Barrier 4: No support network?

It is a lonely existence and nobody takes any interest in your business and ideas.

☐ There are no meetings where you can talk business with other business owners.

☐ There is no one with whom you can discuss or brainstorm business ideas and strategies.

☐ You have nobody with whom to share action plans.

☐ Nobody holds you accountable so your plans often slip behind schedule.

If you ticked two or more of the above, you need Growth Blueprint 3: Build your support network (Chapter 2).

Barrier 5: People problems?

Your employees are not working well together as a team.

- [ ] You have at least one member of staff who consistently underperforms.
- [ ] You don't know whether or not to recruit another member of staff.
- [ ] There is no organisation chart for the business.
- [ ] Staff have no role descriptions.

If you ticked one or more of the above, you need Growth Blueprint 8: Right people (Chapter 4).

Barrier 6: Constantly firefighting?

Your business seems to be in a state of constant crisis management.

- [ ] Employees seem unable to make sensible decisions on their own.
- [ ] You are constantly interrupted and can't get 60 minutes' productive thinking time.
- [ ] You spend most of your time solving problems.
- [ ] You cannot leave the business to operate without constant calls on your mobile phone.

If you ticked one or more of the above, you need Growth Blueprint 17: Stabilise to eliminate firefighting (Chapter 7).

Barrier 7: Letting customers down?

Your business sometimes fails to deliver on quality, time or expectations.

- [ ] Customers are not kept up to date with their orders or service.
- [ ] Deliveries are often late or incomplete.
- [ ] Attention to detail is often lacking.
- [ ] Customers have been lost in the past year due to poor service.

If you ticked one or more of the above, you need Growth Blueprint 20: Essential service for satisfied customers (Chapter 8)

Barrier 8: No idea what marketing works?

Marketing is not measured by counting and capturing the leads it produces.

☐ Intuition or convenience is used to decide where and how to advertise.

☐ Cost per customer is unknown for each marketing campaign.

☐ People who call/visit without buying do not leave their contact details.

☐ There is no regular marketing to a database of prospects.

If you ticked one or more of the above, you need Growth Blueprint 10: Lead capture marketing (Chapter 5).

Barrier 9: Busy, but making no profit?

Business is brisk but there seems to be very little profit.

☐ Prices are set via a margin on costs.

☐ Supplier costs have not been reviewed in the last 12 months.

☐ You have never taken a close look at profit margins.

☐ Overall profit is hurt by a small number of difficult jobs or customers.

If you ticked one or more of the above or want to improve profit margins, you need Growth Blueprint 5: Robust profit margins (Chapter 3).

Barrier 10: No business plan?

There's no real direction for the business.

☐ A long-term aim for the business is missing.

☐ Strategies for growth are unclear.

☐ Employees behave as they see fit personally.

☐ Some short-term goals would focus how much gets done each quarter.

If you ticked one or more of the above, you need Growth Blueprint 7: One-page growth plan (Chapter 4).

Barrier 11: Teamwork could be stronger?

Your employees are not a strong, supportive team.

☐ You feel unsure of yourself as the leader for your business.

☐ Staff are not engaged in improving the business.

☐ Team meetings are irregular and not focused on business growth.

☐ There are conflicts and relationship issues between team members.

If you ticked one or more of the above, you need Growth Blueprint 9: Build a winning team (Chapter 4).

Barrier 12: Customers don't seem very loyal?

Customers are price-sensitive; loyalty seems hard to earn.

☐ Staff rarely smile or make eye contact with customers.

☐ Staff don't really seem to care too much about customers.

☐ Customers treat your business like a commodity item, buying on price alone.

☐ You're stuck for ideas to improve customer service.

If you ticked one or more of the above, you need Growth Blueprint 21: Premium service creates customer loyalty (Chapter 8).

Barrier 13: Lazy salespeople?

Sales performance is poor; there's no sense of structure to the way the salespeople operate.

☐ Salespeople often sell less than they cost the business.

☐ Salespeople are left to manage themselves.

☐ Sales leads are all held on paper or in the heads of salespeople.

☐ Sales follow-up is all rather random and chaotic.

If you ticked one or more of the above, you need Growth Blueprint 15: Sales activity management (Chapter 6).

Barrier 14: Your business doesn't stand out?

There's no clearly articulated unique selling point for your products and services.

☐ Advertising is aimed at anybody who wants to buy; there is no specific target market.

☐ Your business sells more or less the same products and services as its competitors.

☐ You do not think it is possible to offer a money-back guarantee with your products.

☐ You compete for new business mainly on price.

If you ticked one or more of the above, you need Growth Blueprint 11: Make your business stand out (Chapter 5).

Barrier 15: No financial targets?

The business operates without sales or profit targets.

☐ Annual revenues are not planned, but reviewed in hindsight.

☐ Costs are reviewed only when something changes.

☐ Financial goals are set loosely for the year as a general guesstimate.

☐ A bad month's sales catch you by surprise sometimes.

If you ticked one or more of the above, you need Growth Blueprint 6: Realistic sales forecast and budget (Chapter 3).

Barrier 16: Do your adverts really work?

You have no idea what causes most of your advertising to produce zero enquiries.

☐ Adverts feature the name of your business in big letters at the top of the page.

☐ Adverts feature a list of uninteresting bullet points and your phone number at the bottom.

☐ Adverts focus on your products and your firm.

☐ Your adverts offer a free quote or a free consultation.

If you ticked one or more of the above, you need Growth Blueprint 12: Magnetise your marketing (Chapter 5).

Barrier 17: Learnt to sell?

Many sales opportunities seem to slip away as near misses.

☐ Recruiting salespeople is difficult and very hit and miss.

☐ Salespeople are expected to know how to sell, it's their job.

☐ Salespeople frequently discount to make sales, hurting margins.

☐ Salespeople focus exclusively on new sales, not existing customers.

If you ticked one or more of the above, you need Growth Blueprint 16: Create high-performance salespeople (Chapter 6).

Barrier 18: Need more leads and enquiries?

There just aren't enough enquiries coming in for the business to grow.

☐ Word-of-mouth marketing is all that's really working to generate new business.

☐ Lead volumes are inadequate to double your business.

☐ You want to know the best ways to generate new business.

If you ticked one or more of the above and you have funds available to invest in marketing, you need Growth Blueprint 13: Top ten marketing channels (Chapter 5).

Barrier 19: Can't take a holiday without things grinding to a halt?

You are too heavily involved in the day-to-day operation of the business.

☐ Employees forget important actions.

☐ Daily/weekly procedures are sometimes forgotten.

☐ New staff take months to learn how things are done.

☐ People are blamed when things go wrong.

If you ticked one or more of the above, you need Growth Blueprint 18: Systemise to create your operations manual (Chapter 7).

Barrier 20: Selling just one product or service?

You rely on new lead generation because once customers have bought, there is nothing else to sell them for a long time.

☐ The business makes only one-off sales to customers.

☐ There is a constant drive for new customers – past customers are largely ignored for marketing.

☐ The business has no other products to sell to customers.

If you ticked one or more of the above, you need Growth Blueprint 14: A back-end to boost sales (Chapter 5).

Barrier 21: Do inefficiencies squeeze your profits?

You believe your business could run more efficiently and produce even more profit.

☐ There seems to be a lot of material, time or effort wasted in normal operations.

☐ There are lots of repetitive tasks in the business.

☐ Productivity varies from day to day and depends upon circumstances.

☐ It's likely that more profits could be squeezed out with some smart thinking.

If you ticked one or more of the above, you need Growth Blueprint 19: Optimise your business for efficiency (Chapter 7).

Barrier 22: Why don't customers tell their friends about you?

Your customers tell you they love what you do, but produce very few referrals.

☐ There are no 'Wow!' moments for your customers.

☐ People don't rave about your business to their friends.

☐ Customer feedback is positive but ordinary – there's no excitement there.

☐ No one has ever entered the business and said that a friend referred them to you.

If you ticked one or more of the above, you need Growth Blueprint 22: Peak service produces customer referrals (Chapter 8).

Cultivate your habits of success

The Growth Blueprints for self-mastery

Nothing is impossible; the word itself says, 'I'm possible!'
Audrey Hepburn

How much growth did your business achieve during the last year? How much would it have grown if Duncan Bannatyne had been running it? Has somebody somewhere managed to achieve double the success that you have achieved so far, in the same time? The answer will undoubtedly be, 'Yes'. Bill Gates, Warren Buffet, Sir Richard Branson, Charles Dunstone – the list is endless. If one of these people was running your business now, they would have taken it further than you have managed because they bring different habits and skills with them.

The ability to succeed in life is not a trait that people are born with, but something we acquire and can nurture throughout our lives. I cringe when I hear somebody say, 'You can't teach an old dog new tricks' because they are wrong. Having worked with some incredibly successful people, who have built extraordinary businesses, I have noticed that the most successful are often not the most educated or academic, nor the cleverest, but they have several traits that together help them to achieve huge results. This is so important that it's worth stating again, more clearly.

To be successful in business you do not have to be brilliant, but you do need to develop and apply the right habits for success.

So, if intelligence is not the answer, what is?

It turns out that, for at least the last 100 years, bookshelves have become littered with books on the subject of personal achievement and the secrets of success. Perhaps the most famous of these are Napoleon Hill's *Think and Grow Rich* and Stephen R. Covey's *The 7 Habits of Highly Effective People*. Both of these books have sold in their millions and suggest habits that you can adopt to achieve success. Both books, though, suggest so many changes that, it seems, people struggle to use them effectively, which is how this chapter can help.

Here you will find three key principles for your self-mastery that will help you immensely in business. They are fundamental to success and are covered in the following three business Growth Blueprints.

- **Growth Blueprint 1: Get your mojo back!** Knowing what you want to achieve and having the self-belief and passion to stay on course until you achieve it.

- **Growth Blueprint 2: Get organised and focused** Identify and ruthlessly prioritise the most important tasks, ignore distractions and take action to constantly move forwards towards your goals.

- **Growth Blueprint 3: Build your support network** Have a supportive group of friends and colleagues outside of your business to provide a sounding board for ideas and offer external support and motivation when needed.

Many people are afraid of change and, perhaps, you are worried about changing, too. If you like the way you are but are afraid of what you might become, relax a little. Just think back to the very first mobile phone you ever owned. If it was anything like mine, it was a perfectly adequate phone and you were quite happy with it. My first mobile phone did not have e-mail, a camera, Internet browser or even a voice recorder and I did not worry about it, thinking I just wanted a phone that made phone calls – why would anybody want to make it more complicated than that? I was slow to make the change to a smartphone, but now I find the extra features indispensable and frequently use it to send e-mails, check my diary, take photos, etc. In fact, I cannot imagine going back to my old phone now.

Success tip

Think about changing yourself as making a 'personal upgrade' to add some new features or abilities. In this way, you can gradually unlock the potential of your 'inner entrepreneur' and make so much happen without ever losing your sense of identity.

Growth Blueprint 1: Get your mojo back!

My Dad used to say, 'My get up and go has got up and gone!' 'Get up and go' is the perfect description of what is meant by your 'mojo'.

Perhaps you have become burnt out thanks to a combination of never-ending problems, long hours and working at weekends. Perhaps you have become frustrated by the difficulty of trying to make your business grow and feel that whatever you try, nothing ever works. Maybe you've never really had much enthusiasm in the first place, having come into the business thanks to decisions in which you played no active part (this is surprisingly common in family businesses).

To succeed you have to believe in something with such a passion that it becomes a reality.
Dame Anita Roddick, founder of The Body Shop.

Whatever your aim, it must be something that is at the very heart of why you are in business – an essential goal that makes you get out of bed on the coldest winter mornings and energises you to work late just to get things finished. This is mojo. It can send you searching on the Internet for a clever marketing idea – it's probably mojo that made you buy this book.

Yet mojo has an elusive quality and if you suffer a series of setbacks and problems, it's easy for your enthusiasm to fade and for you to settle into a dull routine of working for yourself rather than feel the pride and excitement of building a growing business.

So, let's take a look at how you can reignite your mojo and get that fire in your belly glowing bright and hot.

Are you in the right business?

Building your business is a long game; it's not something that will be done in a few weeks or even a year. You need to have enough interest and enthusiasm to sustain you, to drive your business through the tough times that come to us all – after all, it's very difficult to stay dedicated to a plan if you don't have any interest in it above financial rewards. You'll be less likely to do the tough things if you only want the money and you will fail utterly to inspire your staff to deliver exceptional service if your focus is just on earning a fast buck.

You've got to find what you love. And that is as true for your work as it is for your lovers. Your work is going to fill a large part of your life, and the only way to be truly satisfied is to do what you believe is great work. And the only way to do great work is to love what you do. If you haven't found it yet, keep looking. Don't settle. As with all matters of the heart, you'll know when you find it. And, like any great relationship, it just gets better and better as the years roll on. So keep looking until you find it. Don't settle.

Steve Jobs

So, what if you're in business and find that you don't really care much about what you do? There are three broad options.

1 If you were fired up about your business in the past, but the years of firefighting or struggling to make a decent living have worn it out of you, then it's likely that it will come back as you get control of other areas. If this is you, don't worry about the passion for now; just write a clear list of all the problems that, once cleared, will take you back to those happy days.

2   If you just run the business and have never been passionate about it, you might be able to find something that can fire your passions – like team building maybe. If this doesn't work for you, consider recruiting a general manager to run the business for you, leaving you free to focus on something that *does* get you fired up.

3   Finally, if you really don't like your business much at all, you need to find a way to get out. One client found that having a 12-month goal to stabilise his business and prepare it for a profitable sale was a hugely motivating vision. It got him working harder than ever before and resulted in real sales growth, plus a reigniting of his passion for the business – a true revelation for him. It's the same motivation as the energy people seem to get when they prepare their house for a sale – a powerful short-term motivation to get things right and then move on.

A healthy balance

A business under pressure can often lead to sacrifices being made in other important areas of your life. You spend long hours at work and stop going to the gym. You don't find time to go to the park with your kids because you're too busy finishing off your VAT return. You miss meals and, instead, pick up chocolate bars when you stop for petrol. A steady decline begins with a few decisions to try and put more hours into your business. Slowly your business takes little bites out of your physical health. After a while, your business manages to steal those extra hours forever, putting your life out of balance, leaving you tired, lethargic, grumpy and generally feeling under the weather.

In order to have an energetic and positive mind, your body needs to be energetic, too. Eating well, sleeping well and taking regular exercise are not only commonsense actions but also important factors for the success of your business. The state of your body dictates the state of your mind; the state of your mind dictates the quality of your thinking. When you are tired and run down, you become depressed and lose faith in yourself, you start to make poor decisions and feel sorry for yourself and angry with the world. You stop believing in yourself and your business and, before you know it, your mojo is lost.

Modern research has shown that mild exercise for half an hour a day is at least as effective a treatment for depression as the best antidepressant drugs, but how many people would rather pop a pill a day instead of taking their dog – or themselves – for a decent walk? It is vital for your own and your business' success to create time several days a week to look after yourself. Treat it as a priority – don't miss it today and promise to do extra tomorrow, because tomorrow never comes.

Next, you need to get enough sleep. One of the commonest forms of torture used in war is sleep deprivation. When our son was very young and was ill, we went for three nights straight with no more than an hour or two of sleep each night. Mentally, I was all over the place, literally driven to tears at times by the need for more sleep.

In business, you cannot afford to lose sleep – it will kill your moods, your productivity and your future. Try going to bed an hour or two earlier than usual and don't set an alarm clock. Allow yourself to wake up naturally to prove that your body is getting enough sleep.

You probably didn't expect a book called *Double your business* to tell you how to live, yet, if you are missing your mojo, it's a massively important factor. You need to live more healthily to maximise your energy levels. The pressures of running a business can so easily lead to unhealthy behaviours in terms of diet, smoking, drinking and exercise. The irony is that these are done as pressure-releasing activities, but they have the opposite effect. Making the effort to improve your health will help with your business, too.

Walking to the office every day or walking the dog for 30 minutes in the evening can give your brain valuable freewheeling time and your body a chance to recharge itself. One of my clients had given up going to the gym because of the time demands of her business. Putting the gym back into her schedule on three mornings each week made a profound difference for her. Not only did she feel healthier, she felt far more positive mentally, too. A month after starting, she told me how much more energy she had for business and how much her output had increased.

Success tip

The brain sleeps in cycles of approximately 90 minutes. Set your alarm so that you will get 4, 5 or 6 cycles of 90 minutes each, depending how much sleep you tend to need. If your alarm wakes you midcycle, your brain chemistry can be disturbed at the wrong time, leaving you feeling tired and out of kilter, even if you've had a long sleep overall.

Positive mental attitude

Henry Ford once said, 'If you believe you can, or you believe you can't, you are probably right'. Everybody has dreams of what they want their business to achieve, but only a few have the real belief in themselves to reach their goals. You must develop a positive mental attitude to keep your self-belief going strong.

Steven Callahan was sailing solo when his yacht was badly damaged one night, causing him to abandon ship. He got safely off the boat and on to his life raft, then managed to survive alone at sea for 76 days. During this time, he ate raw fish he caught from the sea, seabirds he trapped on his life raft and drank only the water he could collect with survival techniques he learnt from a book taken from his damaged yacht before he had to abandon it.

The full story is incredible as a feat of endurance and survival (his book *Adrift* is worth reading), but, more than that, his unwavering positive mental attitude, against all the odds, is startling. He never lost hope that, by surviving one day at a time, he would eventually be rescued or reach land. During his time living on the life raft, despite being attacked by a shark and having to fix a puncture with string and a cork, he did whatever it took to survive. This determination – to do things you have never done before, face the unknown and keep fighting with a positive spirit – is what is meant by a positive mental attitude.

In a business that is facing desperate measures, the owner has two choices: to face up to the issues and deal with them, however tough the decisions that must be made, or sit and complain about how unfair life is, how badly he or she is being treated and how somebody else is to blame for all the problems.

During the banking collapse that started in 2007, banks and building societies cut right back on loans and made it impossible for firms to survive. A business owner caught in this could have criticised the failure of government to act more decisively, blamed the banks for the damage they were doing to the business, complained about sales staff not being good enough and watched the business sink, feeling like a helpless victim of the situation (I actually saw several firms go this way).

Meanwhile, one of my clients, although shocked by the turn of events, was very quick to take drastic action. The company shrank the staff numbers and cut fixed costs massively, reducing the business to 50 per cent of its former size within a matter of months. Rather than wallowing in self-pity, the directors took action to save their business by making it leaner and more efficient. They then moved on to start other businesses, using the change in market conditions as an opportunity to take stock of opportunities they had been thinking of for a while. One of those businesses, involved in Internet marketing, is now achieving sales that will see it surpass £1 million per annum in less than a couple of years.

Self-start and take action

Nothing happens in your business until you take action. Great ideas, plans and inspiring talks all have their place, but no results will happen until the work gets done. You need to be in the habit of doing more than talking – of taking action instead of thinking. The most successful people in many fields are the ones who consistently turn ideas into actions.

This tendency towards action means you get to try out more ideas and see which ones work. The more ideas you test, the more you'll know which ones will work. Thomas Edison famously tested thousands of different materials for use as filaments in light bulbs, including 6000 different variations of burnt plants alone, before he found one that worked. So, to become successful, make sure you spend your days working on things that get results, not just daydreaming about what it would be like to get there.

By now you'll appreciate that this first Growth Blueprint is all about you and your attitudes to business and life. As the leader of your business, it will follow where you take it – either up or down – the decision rests with you.

Success tip

You will achieve far more with mediocre goals and massive action than with massive goals and mediocre action.

Breakthrough Action Plan 1: Get your mojo back!

These steps outline some ways to get yourself moving.

1 **Are you in the right business?** Determine some aspect of your business that you can be passionate about. Spend time thinking about this in a deep and concentrated way, to make it real for you.

2 **Healthy balance** Look after yourself so you are in tip-top condition to look after your business. A healthy active body leads to a healthy active mind.

   ■ Rebalance your eating by avoiding sweets, crisps and fast foods as alternatives to real meals. Create enough space to at least eat a sandwich, even when you are busy.

   ■ If you enjoy drinking alcohol, cut back to a level that won't cloud your thinking the next day.

   ■ Exercise regularly. Start now and plan to take at least one brisk 20-minute walk this week.

■ Allow yourself adequate sleep to re-energise. Plan your sleep using the 90-minute cycles to ensure that you get the most from your sleep.

3 **Positive mental attitude** Take ownership of your life and the situation you are in. Instead of blame, decide on the actions you will take to change things for yourself.

4 **Self-start and take action** Write down five little things that you can do to improve your behaviour or your business. Take action on at least one of these every day for the next week. Feel good about achieving something.

Growth Blueprint 2: Get organised and focused

If you want to double your business, you need to make time to do it. If your first thought is, 'I don't have time!', you are in good company. Around one in three business owners/managers will tell you that they don't have time to do anything more, they are just too busy every day. My woodworking teacher at school used to extol the virtues of using sharp tools, explaining that a few minutes every hour to sharpen chisels and plane blades meant that more work got done. He was fanatical about using sharp tools because they cut more accurately, more quickly and less dangerously. You can apply the same idea in business, recognising that more gets done if you step back from the work occasionally and take time to organise yourself and get sharply focused.

Despite the popular phrase 'time management', it's not possible to manage time at all. We all get the same amount of time as each other, but what you choose to do with your time will determine your results. You must be crystal clear not only about the projects you choose to do, but also the ideas and projects you will sacrifice in order to be successful.

There are just five simple things required for high productivity and effective self-management. Once you get yourself organised, by all means try out some different tools to see if you like them, but recognise that what holds you back is your own ability and commitment to stick to the system you choose or create. Here are the five elements:

- action plan
- diary
- filing system
- regular review and ruthless prioritisation
- distraction elimination.

Action plan

Experiments show that we can remember between five and nine ideas in our heads at any one time. Mind you, there are times when I can't even remember what I went upstairs for or where I put the keys! Using a 'to do' list extends your memory on to a piece of paper, taking the burden of recall away from a brain that's not well suited to remembering long lists of things. All you have to remember then is to refer to your list when deciding what to do next. There is also a wonderful sense of satisfaction when you finish a task and can draw a line through it.

A smart way to work is to use two lists – a master list with everything on it and a daily action plan for each day. When something new comes in, if it is important, add it to your master list, unless it must be dealt with today. When writing a daily action plan, leave room for some unexpected items to be added. A good rule of thumb is to put no more than three to five items on each day, leaving room for the unexpected, along with the general needs of your business. Obviously, if there are smaller items, they can be added as quick to do items, too.

Success tip

Even with the best intentions, from time to time it is likely that you will lose control of your to do list and find yourself in a mess. When this happens, don't beat yourself up or abandon your system, simply recognise that you need to 'sharpen your tools'. Spend 15–30 minutes getting in control again by clearing your desk, reviewing your priorities and updating your master list. When you are back in control, write a new daily action plan based on whatever is most valuable for your business.

Diary

You need to be able to organise your time for appointments and meetings, plus plan time for doing important jobs so that they don't get forgotten. There is no hard and fast rule about whether you should use paper or electronic diaries. The secret is to pick one and then stick to it for everything, both business and personal. This makes sense because you only have 24 hours per day and the risk of double-booking increases exponentially with every different calendar you need to update.

Choose the technology that is the best for you – it is a very personal choice. I have clients who use the diary in their customer relationship management system, while others use Microsoft Outlook, Google Calendar or paper diaries. The one thing they have in common, though, is using a *single* diary for *everything*.

If you stop and think about your typical day, you should notice that there are some parts of the day when you feel really energised and other parts when you feel tired. For most people, they feel great during the mid-morning and sleepy after their lunch break (because the body's energy is taken up digesting food). Make sure that the time you block out in your diary for working on Growth Blueprints is the time when your brain is most active.

One of my clients blocks out an hour every morning at 10 for doing her Growth Blueprints work, closing her office door and letting employees know that she is not to be disturbed except in an emergency. In this way she dedicates a predictable five hours every week to improving her business. It was no surprise to me that her business more than doubled in the first year we worked together, because she built her growth time into her diary on a daily basis.

Filing system

You need to be able to find things when you need them and to know where to put new things that you receive. Your filing system must be able to cope with both electronic and paper notes. The simplest way to organise your files is to use hanging files for each major topic. Within each file, use manila folders for storing papers relating to each subtopic.

Some people like to use a numbering system for files, others prefer names. There are no rules here for what's best, just choose what works for you. Some people will tell you that their system is the best, but there's no evidence that any one system is better than any other. As with all the advice in this section, find something that you feel committed to using in the long term and just get on with it. If you don't like the way it works the first time you set it up, you can always change it again in a month's time.

Finally, you need a set of desktop filing trays to gather papers in for quick access. Again, you must label the trays to suit your own needs. A good starting set might be trays labelled 'Inbox', 'Work-in-progress', 'Reading', 'Filing', 'Expenses', 'Outbox'. It is important to set things up in a way that feels right to you. Once each week, review your trays and deal with anything that needs filing. When something is put into a tray or the filing system that has an action associated with it, make sure you add the action to your master list or daily action plan before moving on or else you may forget the action altogether.

Success tip

Review the contents of your trays at least once a week to keep on top of them. If you discover that one is close to overflowing, it's time to 'sharpen the tools' once more. Allocate an hour and go through, making decisions quickly to get back in control. By limiting yourself to an hour, you will be amazed at how quickly you will make decisions.

Regular reviews and ruthless prioritisation

There's a saying that a rocking horse keeps very busy but doesn't get anywhere. The same is true for many people in business. They have so many ideas and start so many projects that they spend all of their time jumping from one to the next, never finishing any of them.

You can only do one thing well at a time, no matter how gifted you are. Trying to run several projects together is a recipe for delays and lost profits.

---

case notes

My client Ian discovered this the hard way. Over the course of a year, he tried 16 different ideas. Yes, 16 of them. Each time he came up with another new idea, it was going to be the big thing to transform his business. Yet, within a few weeks, the grand scheme would be pushed aside for the next big idea.

When we wrote down all of his projects, he realised that each of them had the potential to produce good returns, but all of them needed at least a month or two of dedicated effort. Predictably, none had been delivered in over 12 months of trying. Helping him to focus on one thing at a time made a huge difference. In a further six months, his business had added almost 50 per cent in turnover and even more in profit.

Becoming successful requires you to sacrifice some of your ideas. There is simply not enough time to do it all. So, you have to make tough decisions about which of your ideas has the best chance of success and then give it priority.

One way to set priorities is to assess ideas using factors such as the value of the profit they will produce, the time it will take to deliver them and the cost of getting them done. Everything else gets parked until this project is delivered. To do this you need to have a regular review of your priorities. Look through all of your opportunities and estimate the effort required to deliver them. Choose the projects or ideas that will bring the biggest benefits most quickly. Once you have set your priorities, get to work and make sure that you maintain focus for the time needed to achieve results.

If you have three projects or ideas (A, B, C) and deal with them one after another, rather than trying to do them all at once, you will gain the benefits from them more quickly. Figure 2.1 shows what happens when you try to push just three ideas along at the same time:

Figure 2.1 What happens when you try to progress several ideas at a time

By cycling from one to the next, no results are delivered until some point way in the future. Being successful in business is about delivering results, so this is just the wrong way to do things. Add in two other factors of this type of behaviour and you can see how it goes wrong.

- **The multitasking overhead** Changing from project to project probably adds 20–50 per cent more time to each of them, as you have to catch up with each one every time you pick it up.

- **Extra projects will slide in** Every time I have seen somebody trying to run multiple projects at once, a new project will be added every month or two. Imagine the above diagram with projects D, E, and F added to it. Nothing would ever get finished and the core business would be neglected in favour of the latest great idea.

Yet, if you tackle them in the order A, B, C, you will quickly produce results from your ideas and incrementally improve your business, as shown in Figure 2.2.

Figure 2.2 It is best to tackle projects in order

If you work in this way, there are several benefits that are worth highlighting.

- **Lower costs** Since each project requires some investment (time and materials), running many in parallel is a recipe for cash flow and time management problems. Yet, running one at a time delivers benefits sooner, releasing more cash into your business faster.

- **Produce more profit** If each project, when delivered, will release more profit into your business, then finishing them as quickly as possible will maximise your profit.

- **Momentum and satisfaction** Everybody enjoys success and the sense of progress that comes from completing projects. In the second diagram, success follows success, with work being rewarded faster and more regularly. Your staff would far prefer celebrating finishing a project every few months instead of grinding away at many things for years without ever finishing one of them.

Of course, in practice, you are likely to have many more than three projects or ideas on the go at once. The more ideas you try to multitask, however, the longer it takes for any of them to get finished.

Distraction elimination

If you are constantly interrupted, your concentration is broken before you can get things done and the quality of output will be consistently below your potential. To overcome this you need to establish some rules and habits to prevent your productivity being ruined by distractions.

One great way to do this is to set specific times of the day when your staff are not allowed to interrupt and ask questions, unless there is a serious problem. Educate your staff so they understand what you mean by 'serious' and you can quickly regain control over your time. This will eliminate all sales calls – apart from those who are smart enough to call back at the times you specify – and you will get lots more time to work on growth. Try these three ways to enforce this.

- If you have an office door, close it for the time you need to work without interruption. Tell staff that when the door is closed, they are to wait until it is open again before coming in (or have them ask your deputy, if you have one).
- If your business has a secretary or administrator, ask them to hold all calls and interruptions at these times.
- If phone calls are a constant source of interruption for you personally, get somebody else to take your calls. If there is nobody within the business who can take your calls, consider using an outside call answering service to take messages. Do make sure that those calls are answered by a real person, though – you don't want to lose a customer because they don't like voicemail.

If there is no time during the normal working day when you can work without distractions and no way to eliminate the interruptions, shift your day so that you get in an hour earlier and spend this time developing your business. Sacrificing this first hour to improve your business for a few months can help you to change the way the business works, so that you are no longer needed all day. It is rare that an extra hour is necessary, but in some businesses where the operations are totally dependent upon you, it can be the only realistic way to break out of the cycle which has resulted in the business sitting on your back. Simply put, you need to find time to do your double your business activities. Just remember that this hump of extra work is required before you get to enjoy the rewards.

Breakthrough Action Plan 2: Get organised and focused

Follow the simple plan below to gain control of your business life.

1 Create a master list, choose a diary and prepare your filing system (as set out in Growth Blueprint 2).

2 Clear your workspace into your filing system. Each time you identify something that needs an action, add it to your master list.

3 Review your master list and, for each item, ask yourself these questions.

- Will it help you to grow your business or is it business as usual?
- What other projects or actions do you need to start to grow your business?
- What is the single most valuable project to work on? Put this at the top of your master list.
- Are there any quick win ideas/projects that you can do right away that will provide a good return immediately?

4 Add any newly identified growth actions to your master list.

5 Block out times in your diary for:

- your business growth actions – choose a time for this when you are at your sharpest mentally and alert
- other regular actions, such as staff meetings, financial reviews, etc.
- actions you need to do regularly but forget!

6 Deal with interruptions by training your team to store up questions and problems to bring to you at specific times each day or week.

Growth Blueprint 3: Build your support network

Running a small business can be a lonely activity. When your spouse or partner has no interest in the business, it is not uncommon to feel very isolated. While the top person in a corporation is supported by a management team inside his or her own organisation, owners of small businesses need to look outside their own business for support. Your support network is like an extended family, but with one special advantage – you get to choose the members!

American success coach Jim Rohn once said, 'You are the average of the 5 people you spend the most time with'. If you want to be more successful, make sure you link up with people who will stretch you to grow and reach another level.

Highly successful people attract at least as many detractors and negative comments as they do admirers. Those negative people will have failed to achieve their own potential and excuse themselves for it, so they become bitter about those who excel. Time spent with bitter and negative people can rub off as bitterness and negativity on you. Avoid it at all costs. If this means you need to find some new friends and move away from some unhelpful relationships, then what are you really losing if all they do is to drag you down?

Success tip

Negative people are sometimes described as 'energy vampires' – they drain your energy and enthusiasm. If you find that contact with them is unavoidable (often the case with negative family members), find ways to limit your personal exposure to them – make meetings every fortnight instead of weekly, meet for coffee instead of dinner, focus on the positive people at the same meetings, etc.

At the same time, a good support network will include somebody who is able to take a critical look at what you are doing and take the role of devil's advocate. While the devil's advocate can be frustrating, this role provides the checks and balances that force your own critical thinking to engage, improving the quality of your results.

There are several different ways to build an effective support network in this Growth Blueprint.

Books, DVDs and CDs

Getting direct personal access to people like Sir Richard Branson is difficult, if not impossible, but there are autobiographies and other literature written by them and about them that provide insights into their thinking and behaviours. Through learning about their successes and the obstacles they overcame, your own thinking can be changed and improved.

If you have particular favourite personalities who have become very successful, try to get closer to them by watching and listening to them presenting or being interviewed. Reading the things they have published can give further inspiration.

> ### Success tip
>
> YouTube, TED.com and Twitter provide direct exposure to some super-achievers. As well as practical tips and talks on YouTube and inspirational speeches on TED, Twitter offers the chance to hear their views on the world. Notice how they will avoid the negative, even replying forcefully against criticism that is aimed at them.

At the back of this book is a section entitled 'Further reading'. There are some inspiring books listed there, written about or by highly successful entrepreneurs, as well as ones by successful people from other walks of life.

Networking events, business exhibitions and conferences

Business owners benefit a great deal from interacting with other people in business. This is called business networking and a good place to start is your local Chamber of Commerce. Such organisations hold meetings, probably monthly, with members drawn from a variety of business types. Go along as a visitor for a meeting or two and see if it would benefit you to join.

The Internet search engines are your friend for getting started – simply search for 'business networking Bristol', or whatever your town is, and you will find a range of groups. Having attended one, let people know you are new to networking and they will suggest other suitable groups and recommend their own favourites.

With networking events, the benefit is often not directly from the meeting itself, but the relationships that are formed by attending. Don't judge the value of networking solely on the value produced for your bottom line, but include the benefits of the relationships you build, too.

Another idea is to watch for conferences. Apart from the obvious benefit of hearing the content from expert speakers, conferences also offer lots of social time to engage with other attendees. Mix around these events and try to identify people of interest to you. Some of them may want to keep in touch afterwards and you can form an informal support network for each other – precisely what you are looking for.

If you have a specific business problem relating to the topic of a conference, that can be a big help in getting to know people. For instance, if you wanted to know whether or not to upgrade your computer software to the latest version or how to get better results from e-mail marketing, you could wander through a conference related to these topics asking people what their experience has been.

Success tip

It is common to hear that attendees get more value from the people they meet at conferences and training events than the formal presentations. The people you meet can often provide insights to business growth from their own experiences that can act like a short cut to success.

Online networking and social networks

'Online networking' is the phrase used to describe the use of community websites, including Facebook and Twitter. These sites provide a place for friends to 'chat' with one another, share experiences and links to other pages of interest. After creating a free account, users fill out a profile page to describe themselves and then interact with other members. They then choose appropriate groups and forums to join within the sites and participate by introducing themselves, asking questions, answering questions and generally joining in the chitchat.

While sites such as Facebook and Twitter have grabbed most of the headlines concerning online networking, there are many other places to find business friends online and begin collaborating with them. The most significant of these places is LinkedIn – a networking site that is specifically designed to support business and career relationships. While these sites are useful for marketing, they are also a powerful place to build supportive and collaborative relationships.

As well as these large, international sites, there are many online forums that serve a narrower membership, with topics ranging from individual business areas, like managing people or sales skills, through to more general small business forums. The most active of these sites are busy meeting places for many business owners/managers.

Let me give you an example of just how useful these sites can be. When a client, Richard, broke his laptop screen and needed access to files on his machine, he was helped immediately by members of one business forum. Several people offered advice, but one of them was able to replace the screen and get him running again, all within 48 hours. Access to fast, pertinent help like this is invaluable when you are in business for yourself.

Success tip

Another way to establish a business support relationship is to identify specific individuals who have their own blogs. You can gradually get to know them through reading and commenting on their blog posts. These relationships can be nurtured and developed into a proper support network. I have done this myself and have several friends now that I first came across when commenting on their blogs.

Business coaches and mastermind groups

When more direct support or help is required, including the desire for a regular sounding board, it may be beneficial to consider working with a business coach.

A good coach can provide much of what is required in your support network. While having a sounding board is helpful and being held accountable to get things done ensures increased productivity, there are obviously also real benefits from getting support from advisers who have helped others to achieve similar objectives in the past.

When talking to a coach, the single most important question to consider is, 'Do they focus on results?' Look for strong testimonials – ask to speak to past clients. Many coaches act as sounding boards and are very good at this, but the best will have a track record of helping clients to produce impressive results.

You could also join (or initiate) a mastermind group. This idea was developed by Napoleon Hill in his classic manual for success *Think and Grow Rich*. A mastermind group is a collection of two or more people who meet on a regular basis with the common aim of helping each other to succeed in business. A good group will comprise owners from a range of businesses who have achieved levels of success in different ways. By offering candid advice and opinions, each member takes away far more from the group than they would create on their own.

The idea in each case is the same: to find people who will challenge and stretch your thinking, educate you in the art of what is possible and then hold you accountable to get things done.

Breakthrough Action Plan 3: Build your support network

To build your support network, follow these steps.

1 Take a blank piece of paper and write down the names of the people you spend the most time with each week.

   ■ If you spend a lot of time reading books, watching TV or listening to the radio, they are the people who are influencing you – so who are they? Write down the names of TV programmes, including the news if that's something you watch every single day.

2 Now assess what you have learnt from these sources in the past few months. What do you know, believe or what skill do you now have that

has come directly from your current network? If the results show that your network is teaching you nothing, it's time to change it.

3 Write a list of the skills, knowledge or support you would most like to be getting.

4 Who would be able to help you with these things? Consider:

- other business owners (and what kinds of business they own and what sorts of people they are)
- role models, like super-successful entrepreneurs
- professional advisers
- mastermind groups.

5 Develop a simple plan to get you close to the kinds of people you identified in the previous step. Consider:

- books, DVDs, audio courses
- business networking events
- online groups and forums
- conferences and similar events
- networking meetings
- professional advisers.

6 Now take action! Build your support network and move closer to success.

Key points from this chapter

- Embracing personal change and growth are the precursors to business growth.

- Eliminating the good ideas that you will not pursue is perhaps the biggest secret to achieving focus.

- Expanding your horizons by getting the perspectives of people outside your business will stretch and benefit you enormously.

Understand your accounts to make more money

The Growth Blueprints for financial management

Never spend your money before you have earned it.
Thomas Jefferson

Given that the job of business is to make money, it should come as no surprise to discover that the Growth Blueprints presented in this chapter are profoundly important. If neglected, financial Barriers to Growth can be like daggers striking at the very heart of your business and have you fighting for survival.

When most business owners talk about their accounts, they are referring to the submission that their accountant prepares once a year for tax and legal purposes. Surprisingly few owners seem to appreciate that a basic understanding of figures will provide greater control, confidence and insights that will drive their business forwards.

In this chapter you'll read about the three big financial Growth Blueprints and be able to develop a plan to grow your business. There is nothing complicated about basic accounts – they just use a bit of simple maths. Once you understand a few important terms, you will find that your fear of accounts will evaporate and you will get closer to understanding and controlling your business. Before getting into the Growth Blueprints, though, read this story of a business that was able to increase its profit tenfold within a few days, simply by getting to grips with its accounts.

case notes

Walking into the large commercial unit of Stephen's security business, you could be forgiven for thinking this was the office of a successful business. Stephen had approached me for sales and marketing advice. Arriving on the first day to discuss how we could improve the poor sales performance, I quickly learnt that this firm had a much more serious problem – one Stephen was blind to.

Stephen dug out a copy of the business' annual accounts and we spent a few minutes looking through the figures. Table 3.1 shows what we saw.

Table 3.1   Simplified income statement for Stephen's security business

Sales	£650,000
Cost of goods sold	£455,000
Gross profit	**£195,000**
Total expenses	£183,000
Net profit	**£12,000**

Let's take just a moment to understand these figures.

- **Sales** is the total value of sales that a business makes in a year or month. It's also commonly called *turnover* or *revenue*. In Stephen's business, sales were £650,000 for the year.

- **Cost of goods sold** is the sum of costs incurred when a business makes a sale. It includes materials and any subcontracted labour. It's also sometimes called *cost of sales*. Stephen's total cost of goods sold was £455,000 for the year, which covered the alarm system hardware and materials used during installation, plus the cost of subcontracted engineers.

- **Gross profit** is a calculation showing the difference between the sales and the cost of goods sold. In simple terms, it is the money

▶ that came into Stephen's business during the year after the cost of doing the jobs had been covered.

■ **Total expenses** is the sum of all the bills that have to be paid by a business even when it makes no sales. It typically includes things like pay, rent, rates, utilities, insurances, office supplies, repairs, training, telephones, vans and equipment, etc. It is often also called *fixed costs, overheads* or simply *expenses*.

■ **Net profit** is the profit that's left after the total expenses have been paid. This is what a business is meant to produce – in simple terms, the bigger your net profit, the better your business is doing. To calculate it, simply subtract the total expenses from the gross profit.

From these figures, we can see that Stephen's business made a net profit of just £12,000 from sales of £650,000. Stephen explained that he and his wife were earning just £18,000 between them for working very long hours, some of which was included in the total expenses (their pay) and the rest being claimed as a dividend from the net profit. So, their income from a £650,000 business was just £9000 each – a figure that was less than any of their employees were earning.

Looking at the figures again, they were making £195,000 gross profit from sales of £650,000. That is, just 30 per cent of their sales was coming back as profit (this figure is known as the *gross margin percentage*). It was only just covering their expenses of £183,000.

Stephen was shocked by this and explained that he always quoted using a 55 per cent margin, often higher. Now we had a mystery to solve, because it appeared that 25 per cent of his profit margin was getting eaten up somewhere between quoting for and completing the jobs.

The first thing we did was to work through his quoting method, to make sure that he really was doing it right. A common mistake when pricing products is to confuse mark-up with margin, which is covered later in this chapter. Stephen's job quotes were fine, however, with a solid 55 per cent gross profit planned in from the start. That meant the problem had to lie in the way the jobs were being done, rather than simply being an accounting error.

Fortunately, Stephen kept a job sheet for every installation, recording all the materials used to do the jobs and the hours paid to the installation engineers. After going through the records for the month, it was clear that more than half of the jobs finished late and used extra materials. Engineers were routinely having to come back to base for extra parts or tools that they had forgotten or were buying extra tools local to where they were working when they already had them back at base.

By the time each job was finished, Stephen was paying the engineer for an extra day or two of work, plus overtime, as well as all the extra odds and ends being bought by engineers at retail prices because they had failed to assemble proper toolkits for each job. Almost every job came in below the target profit margin, with many actually losing money. By the time we had finished, it was clear that poor operational systems and management were the root cause of the business' poor margins.

Worse news was to follow, though. Stephen's poor margins meant that the business did not produce enough profit to pay him what he needed to service his mortgage and lifestyle. Despite this, Stephen had continued to draw what he needed from the business, pushing it into overdraft. On top of this, he had leased a brand new car for his salesperson without understanding how much extra sales revenue was required just to pay for the car. The business was running on the brink of disaster, right up to its overdraft limit.

We needed to act fast. By the start of the next day, checklists were introduced to ensure adequate spare parts and full toolkits were kept in the vans to save the engineers having to come back to base halfway through a job, wasting time. Freelance contracting engineers had their terms of employment changed – to a fixed price for a job, rather than a daily rate. The quotation system was changed to increase prices slightly, allowing for a target 60 per cent gross profit margin for each job. Monitoring the performance of these new systems during the next month demonstrated margins were operating at 50 per cent.

That change alone, when considered across a full year, boosted the gross profit from £195,000 to £325,000. That same change did not affect anything else – the business still cost the same to run.

> ▶ This meant that, after subtracting the £183,000 of total expenses, the net profit increased from a very sickly £12,000 to an impressive £142,000 per annum. That's more than a tenfold increase in profit from a change that took just a day to diagnose and a week or two of focused management time to fix.

Many business owners and managers do not understand their finances and we tend to fear what we don't understand. In Stephen's case, the cost of him avoiding his accounts was £130,000 per annum in lost profit.

You cannot afford to give your accountant all of the numbers to deal with in the mistaken belief that the accounts are not important and don't deserve your attention. Your business needs to make money in order to survive and provide an income for you and your family, as well as the people who work for you. Taking the time to know how the numbers of your business work can have a profound impact upon the money you personally make.

The rest of this chapter is given over to the three fundamental financial Growth Blueprints and teaches you how to make more money from your business in less time.

Success tip

To create models and plans for the finances in a business, most people use spreadsheet software, such as Microsoft Excel. To manage your accounts, however, there is no substitute for professional accounting software, which a good accountant will help you to choose and use.

Don't use a lack of understanding of the software as an excuse for not understanding your numbers – learning to use a spreadsheet will take you a few hours and, apart from accountants, there's lots of high-quality free training online to get you started. If this is too tricky for you, get help from your accountant to set things up so that you can review your numbers regularly.

Growth Blueprint 4: Properly managed cash flow

Cash flow is the movement of money in and out of a business. Many profitable businesses have failed because they have not managed their cash flow effectively. Even when you are making a profit, if you don't get paid, the money to keep going dries up and your business dies with it.

In the UK, the Office for National Statistics publishes business survival data that show 53.2 per cent of businesses will fail within 5 years. Practically every list of reasons for business failure puts poorly managed cash flow at the top. From this it is clearly important to understand and manage cash flow – simply so you survive, let alone grow!

There are six common scenarios that can cause your cash flow to run dry. These will be considered in turn to understand how they happen and what to do about them.

Consistently operating below your breakeven sales

The simple truth about any business is that it must bring in more cash than it spends. If a business consistently spends more than it makes, it will run out of money and fail.

The *breakeven sales* figure for a business is the amount of sales required to cover total expenses without making a net profit. It is the minimum sales required just to stay in business. It is normal to calculate breakeven sales on a weekly or monthly basis.

For example, one business had steady sales of £30,000 per month and its total expenses (mostly pay) were £25,000 per month. When a competitor moved in, its sales dropped to £20,000. The owners had great loyalty to their staff and refused to make any redundancies as a matter of principle. Operating at a loss of £5000 per month, however, was unsustainable and, within a year, the business simply ran out of money, costing far more jobs than would have been lost if the owners had acted earlier.

Poor credit control

One manufacturing business had a turnover of £500,000 and about 600 customers who bought from it each year. Its bank account was heavily overdrawn and the owners were under pressure from the bank to reduce their borrowing. The business was achieving strong sales, but admitted that it was supplying some customers who had not paid their previous invoices. A review of unpaid invoices quickly got to the bottom of the issue.

There was £120,000 sitting in the bank accounts of their customers, £80,000 of which was overdue, with much of it being owed for three months or more. The owners immediately set to work on collecting these debts. They hired a part-time bookkeeper to keep track of debtors and put in place a credit control system to chase people with phone calls and letters when payments were due. Within 3 months, the debts had been reduced to just £47,000, putting an extra £73,000 in the business' bank account and taking it out of overdraft.

This business enjoyed making things – it was exceptionally good at product design, manufacture and customer service – but it hated chasing people for money. Introducing effective credit control to chase overdue debts transformed its cash flow and got the business back on track.

Too many bad debts

An engineering business went into liquidation because one of its customers held back payment of several large invoices. The engineering firm had paid the people who did the work, bought the materials and paid for delivery overseas. The debts grew over a two-year period and the debtor, a large multinational business, seemed to have a finance director who liked to play games.

This big debtor continued to place orders, however, and paid for some of them. This made it difficult for the engineering business to stop selling to them, especially as these sales made up over half of its total orders. On paper, *all* of the sales should have been profitable, but, because the business wasn't being paid on time, the cash kept running out. If the engineering firm had taken an order and waited until shipping day, then refused to ship until all outstanding payments were made, they would have been able to force the customer to pay its debts. Instead, it decided to keep shipping to 'keep the customer happy', with disastrous results.

Success tip

To avoid this situation, never rely upon just one or two important customers for a large proportion of your sales. Any customer that represents more than 10–20 per cent of your sales or profit is dangerous because of the impact on your business if they don't pay. If you are in this situation, seek to attract more customers quickly to avoid being held over a barrel and stop supplying the bad debtor until any overdue debts are settled.

Too much cash tied up in unsold stock

Another common situation is when a business that sells products allows old stock to accumulate over the years. After a while, there will be old stock that simply does not sell, yet it cost money to buy in the first place; this depletes the bank account of cash reserves, preventing more up-to-date products from being stocked. With little hope of being sold, the old stock is effectively worthless to a business and serves no valuable purpose.

In one business with an overdraft of £25,000, there was old stock worth in excess of £60,000. When we looked closely at its stock control system, it was clear that most of the stock items had not been sold in the past 12 months, meaning that £60,000-worth of old products had shifted from being stock to becoming a noose around the neck of the business. It had to urgently hold a fire sale and turn this old stock into cash, even at cost price, simply to convert these almost unsaleable items into money in its bank account again.

This strategy of holding a fire sale is a really clever way to quickly clear your stockroom or warehouse of surplus items. You can do this in a number of ways, with an 'invitation only' event proving very successful for some of my past clients – customers feel they're getting a real treat. You can sell the old stock at big discounts or even zero margins just to release the cash so it can go back into your bank. If you have stock that is terribly out of date and unfashionable or difficult to sell, you can consider using an online auction site, local auctions or simply sell it below cost price in a massive promotional sale. You could even do a couple of car boot sales if you are desperate to release cash and have old stock to sell. No matter what you have to sell, there will be somebody out there who will want to buy it.

Insufficient working capital

Accountants have a complicated definition for working capital that relates to the money that is tied up in various stages of production and operations of a business. For example, a builder will use lots of cement, bricks, windows, roofing tiles and so on while building new houses. Until a property is sold, the cost of these materials has to be absorbed in the working capital of the business. If a business does not have sufficient money available to cover this working capital until a product is sold, it will run out of cash.

When an engineering firm won a large new contract to supply aero engine components, it had to spend large sums of money on raw materials. It did not pay attention to the three-month manufacturing cycle of the components and did not have enough money to keep all the work going until it would be paid for delivery. It had to find an investor to help it fund the work, otherwise it would have had to turn the job down.

Be careful when accepting a large new order if your cash flow is weak. If you have to pay your bills before your customer pays you, you may not have sufficient working capital and run into cash flow problems.

Directors/owners drawing too much cash

This one is almost too obvious to mention, yet it's surprisingly common. There is a temptation to take money from a business to fund a lifestyle or pay personal debts. If this is done for too long, the business runs into overdraft and, without increasing sales, it simply does not have the cash to survive.

A landscape gardening business was attracting plenty of fresh business and the teams were constantly busy, yet the bank account was in overdraft and the owner was struggling to pay the bills. A review of the accounts showed that the owner was taking more income from the business than the net profit it was producing.

If this situation sounds familiar, look for other ways to make ends meet at home and give your business the chance to succeed by having the cash it needs to operate and grow.

Breakthrough Action Plan 4: Properly managed cash flow

If you have read through the details for Growth Blueprint 4, you will understand just how important a strong cash flow is to the survival of your business. Follow these steps to gain control.

1 Calculate your breakeven sales value.

- Go back over the last six months and check that every month you exceeded your breakeven point.

- Next, confirm with your salespeople (or your own forecasts) if the next month is likely to exceed your breakeven point.

- If you are failing to break even, create a plan to increase sales and reduce costs.

- If you have salespeople, get them to come up with ideas to increase sales.

2 Get on top of your credit control with a standardised system for collection. One method might be to do this:

- five days before the invoices are due, call the clients to make sure that they have their invoices and have no problems with their orders

- if they have not paid on the day their invoices are due, call to let them know that their payments haven't been received and ask them to confirm when you'll be paid

- a week later, send them a friendly letter to remind them that their payments are overdue and to please pay immediately or arrange terms to pay

- another week later, send a more formal letter and follow this up with a phone call to agree a date for payment

- finally, when the bill is three to four weeks late, send a final warning letter informing them that their account will be passed to your debt collection agency if payment is not received within five working days

- you can increase the impact of these letters by printing them on different colours of paper and by printing a red 'Second warning' and 'Final warning' stamp on the second and third ones

- withhold further deliveries from people who have not paid and insist on payment before you release their orders to them.

3 Manage consistently late payers effectively by asking your accounts people for the details of any late payers, including the sizes of the accounts and numbers of days late. Then:

- contact each of the late payers by phone to discuss their reasons for non-payment

- change your terms and conditions of business to cash on delivery or even payment in advance

- change your terms and conditions to include a late payment surcharge

- wherever possible, get a signature from your customer on a form that states they accept your terms and conditions of business before you start supplying them – this will make debt collection easier if it becomes necessary.

4 Review your biggest suppliers and renegotiate payment terms to increase the duration of credit you receive or agree sale or return terms.

5 Stop supplying customers who are in danger of becoming bad debtors. While it seems unpleasant, the truth is that the more inconvenience your stopping supply causes them, the better the chance that they will pay you this time in order to get their goods.

6 When taking on large orders, forecast your cash flow carefully to take into account working capital and seek extra funds ahead of time to call on if required.

7 Do a stock inventory and determine which items have sat unsold for more than six months. Calculate the value of this stock if it was sold at a 20 per cent or even 30 per cent discount (or ask your accountant to do it). Based on this, you might consider having a fire sale.

8 If you need more working capital due to the nature of your business, you could consider introducing different terms and conditions that provide stage payments or seek investment from outside to give you a healthier bank balance.

9 How much money did your business make in the past three months?

_____

How much money have you drawn from your business in this time?

_____

If you have drawn more money than you made, you need to fix this – fast.

Growth Blueprint 5: Robust profit margins

There is a popular saying in business that turnover is vanity, profit is sanity and cash is king. When a business has a solid sales turnover but not much profit is created, it has poor profit margins. The purpose of any business is to add value through the delivery of products or services in order to make a profit. The more profit that is made, the more money the owner makes. Plus, a profitable business is able to invest for the future, protecting itself in a constantly changing world.

In the example of Stephen's security business at the beginning of this chapter, two types of profit were discussed: gross and net. A simple example is that a speedboat is bought for £100,000 and sold for £150,000 to make a gross profit of £50,000. This assumes that no commission is paid to a salesperson and there are no other costs associated with this sale. From this £50,000 gross profit, the total expenses have to be paid, covering things like showroom rent, staff pay, utilities bills, insurances, etc. After paying for all of these costs, the money left over is net profit.

Improving your profitability is done using two basic methods –

increasing prices and reducing costs. There are lots of ways that both of these can be achieved.

Increase prices

Prices are often set based on some formula based on the cost of materials rather than the value the customer is getting. For example, a designer watch may use the same mechanism inside as an everyday brand. The everyday brand will charge a low price based on its cost of manufacture; the designer brand will charge a premium for putting its name on the watch. The difference between the two is the *perception of value*. If people perceive a product to have a higher value, they will gladly pay a premium for it.

This notion holds true for practically every small business. Except for pure commodity items, there are factors relating to service that can be used to differentiate a business from its competitors. Yet, so many businesses work on the false assumption that they must be cheaper than the competition to survive. This is simply not true. If your service is at least as good as your competitors', your prices should be similar or even higher. Plus, when you can drive your service to even higher levels (which you'll be doing as you work through these Growth Blueprints) you deserve to be paid a premium for them.

An important factor to understand in pricing is the effect on profit. The bigger the difference between the cost of a product and the price it sells for, the higher the profit margin. This often makes discounting a fool's strategy, because it can destroy margins. If a tin of paint costs £10 and normally sells for £20, that will give a gross profit of £10. Applying a discount of 25 per cent reduces the sale price to £15 per tin and the gross profit is cut to just £5. That is because the discount only cuts the profit margin – the paint still costs the same to make. Selling 10 tins previously made a gross profit of £100. After the 25 per cent discount, it is necessary to sell *20* tins just to maintain the *same* profit level.

This shows how discounting can be a fast way to lose money, even when it produces more sales. A smarter strategy is to add value to differentiate products and services from competitors. In the case of the tin of paint, a shop could give away some accessories with each tin, perhaps a disposable paint roller and tray. If these were bought in bulk, they might cost no more than £2 per set. This could be added to the price of the paint. The customers perceive the package of paint *and* roller and tray is better value than buying the paint on its own.

---

case notes

The restaurant

In a busy restaurant that was making little profit, a quick review of the menu showed a wine list with each bottle priced in a narrow range of around £12 to £15. With no higher-priced wines, people simply were not given the choice to spend more.

As the restaurant offered great-quality food, the wine list was rebuilt to offer a wider range in terms of quality, with prices to match. The new menu started at the same £12 per bottle entry level, but went up to £35 or more for nicer wines and good champagnes at £70 per bottle. This was one of several changes made over 12 months and these increased average spend per customer from £15 to £27 – an 80 per cent increase.

The leaflet distributor

The same can be done for all kinds of business. A leaflet delivery business charged £30 per 1000 leaflets posted through letterboxes. When he was told that his prices were too low to ever make a decent profit, the owner calculated that he needed to charge £40 per 1000. He lost a night's sleep worrying about the consequences of this price increase. Yet, when he tested it out on the next ten people who enquired about the service, he found that they gladly paid it for the professional service he was offering. This was a big contributor to his profits doubling within a few short months.

When I have given this same advice to many other service businesses – accountants, solicitors, consultants, therapists and so on – I have seen exactly the same results.

Reduce costs

The second way to improve margins is cost control.

Costs are incurred when making sales (cost of goods sold) and in overall operations (total expenses). There are often savings to be made in both of these areas. Four ways to address these are covered below.

Supplier review

If the same suppliers have been used for years, it's likely that they have gradually pushed up their prices. A review of prices, comparing them with those of other suppliers, can reveal surprising savings. Aim for a saving of 10–20 per cent and ensure that quality is maintained at the lower prices. A financial services firm was able to save 50 per cent from its mobile phone bills by negotiating far better contracts – a saving of £400 per month for just an hour's work. A restaurant saved £1800 by changing the credit card processing company it used – it just took a couple of hours' effort. There are lots of tactics you can apply to reduce costs from suppliers, including bulk purchase deals, minimum order commitments, bonus items, whatever you can get!

Business efficiencies

As a business grows, the way it does things can become overly complicated and wasteful. A property management firm simplified its internal procedures and reorganised its team to be more efficient. It was able to eliminate three members of staff and provide better service, while saving thousands of pounds each month. While cutting staff numbers is never a nice thing to do, it is far better than carrying unnecessary costs as a burden on everybody else.

Unprofitable customers

A review of customers may find that some cost more to service than the profit made from dealing with them. These customers should be eliminated to make room for more profitable ones. One client found that her first 20 customers, who had helped her to establish the business when she worked from home, were paying just half the normal rate for the service. Having moved to an office, this was no longer viable – these customers were costing her money! Asking them to pay the same fees as everybody else eliminated many of them, but boosted profit margins substantially.

Theft

It is surprising how much money can be lost to theft in a small business. Supplies can be stolen by delivery drivers who 'forget' to deliver part of an order; thieves can steal anything, including spare parts, office supplies or simply stock that should be sold to customers. Cash is a very tempting target and must be very carefully managed, using tracking and reconciliation systems.

Wastage

As the business grows and more time is spent serving customers, the value of waste can rise alarmingly. A plastic manufacturing company had a wastage rate of 25 per cent due to poor process management. Spotting this and an hour's brainstorming eliminated the problem altogether, cutting raw materials costs substantially.

Breakthrough Action Plan 5: Robust profit margins

Follow these steps to give your profits a serious boost.

1 Eliminate discounts, except for old stock that you want to offload quickly. Replace discounts on more recent stock with added value to your customers through additional services or add-on products that don't hurt your margins.

2 Make a list of your competitors and what they charge. Compare their prices to your own and then consider increasing your prices – it's the fastest way to increase profit.

3 Negotiate better deals with your suppliers.

4 Review all suppliers and explore savings available by changing. Set a target of saving at least 10 per cent on all suppliers' prices and see if you can beat this, including utilities.

5 Introduce simple procedures to discourage theft and keep it to a minimum:

■ check all deliveries against orders so that you can be sure nothing is going missing

■ track and manage stock with some form of stock control system to monitor stock movements

■ employ systems that produce invoices and receipts that can be used for cash reconciliation in a cash business (ask your accountant for help with this if you're unsure how this should work).

6 Measure waste from any production activities you undertake and set targets to eliminate or minimise wastage so your team understand the value of what gets thrown away.

7 Review your product and service mix and, if necessary, introduce a single, premium product or service to produce higher margins from existing customers.

8 Have monthly management accounts prepared for your business so that you can review margins and costs regularly to maintain your profit levels.

Growth Blueprint 6: Realistic sales forecast and budget

Most small businesses trade from month to month with no specific goals for their sales. Without a clear financial goal, a business tends to trade at more or less the same level of sales from month to month. It's like a footballer kicking a ball to the end of the field with invisible goalposts. Some of the time he will miss, some of the time he will score, but if the posts were visible the success rate would be far greater.

Creating a planned series of sales targets is a way of concentrating efforts on achieving a particular monthly, then annual sales figure. A budget is a similar set of targets for total expenses, helping to rein in spending and maximise net profit for the business. It is created using spreadsheet software and allows you to enter a budget as well as current information.

In the simplified example in Figure 3.1, a shoe shop has sales in three areas: shoes, accessories and repairs.

Sales forecast (sales)	July	August	September	
Shoes	£20,000.00	£18,000.00	£24,000.00	1. Plan for seasonal shifts
Accessories	£1,300.00	£1,200.00	£1,500.00	
Repairs	£900.00	£900.00	£900.00	
Total sales	£22,200.00	£20,100.00	£26,400.00	
Cost of goods sold (CoGS)	July	August	September	
Shoes	£10,000.00	£9,000.00	£12,000.00	
Accessories	£300.00	£280.00	£350.00	
Repairs	£600.00	£600.00	£600.00	
Cost of goods sold total	£10,900.00	£9,880.00	£12,950.00	
Gross profit (sales – CoGS)	£11,300.00	£10,220.00	£13,450.00	
Gross margin (%)	51%	51%	51%	
Total expenses budget	July	August	September	
Staff pay	£6,000.00	£4,500.00	£4,500.00	2. Reduce staff in line with seasonal shifts?
Rent	£950.00	£950.00	£950.00	3. Find cheaper gas and electric
Utilities	£1,000.00	£1,000.00	£750.00	
Mobile phones	£250.00	£100.00	£100.00	4. Shared minutes deal
Total expenses	£8,200.00	£6,550.00	£6,300.00	
Net profit (Gross profit – Expenses)	£3,100.00	£3,670.00	£7,150.00	

Figure 3.1 A sales forecast and budget spreadsheet for a shoe shop

The spreadsheet shown in Figure 3.1 was prepared with an expectation that sales tend to vary each month (1), with a drop in August due to summer holidays and a last-minute rush in September for the start of a new school year. The spreadsheet can be populated by looking at sales figures for previous months and years, so that predictable trends, like seasonal variations, can be taken into account.

After this, the expenses can be reviewed to identify potential savings. In the example given in Figure 3.1, the owner has decided that savings can be made in staff pay (2), utilities (3) and mobile phones (4).

The *actual* performance each month can then be compared to the targets for sales and total expenses. In practice, this comparison drives behaviours to increase sales and reduce expenses, resulting in higher net profit. Obviously, simply changing the figures does not produce the desired results on its own. Action must be taken in order to achieve the growth. The sales forecast and budget is simply a tool to help achieve and maintain momentum towards growth. It also helps the owner or manager to maintain control over spending as, during growth phases, it can be tempting to increase spending without realising the impact on profitability.

---

case notes

When Helen's sales grew by 25 per cent in a matter of months, she was so excited that she began to get a little ahead of herself. In an excited flourish she began to order new uniforms for her team, new computers and phones and invest in all sorts of training courses for herself and her staff. She then complained that, despite the growth in sales, her profit had fallen slightly.

When we took the time to go through her accounts, it was very clear that the growth had given Helen the confidence to spend more money, but, without any method to control her spending, she was spending too much. Helen had also hired new staff as soon as her business grew a little. This meant that she was spending all new profit on additional costs incurred by hiring new staff and buying new equipment. Once she understood what was going on by using a sales forecast and budget spreadsheet, she was able to plan sales and expenses effectively and this substantially improved her overall profits.

When you have a goal to make a certain amount of money during the year, you can adjust your sales and costs within the spreadsheet to accurately plan how you will achieve your profit goal. Just remember to only write things that you are totally committed to achieving – otherwise this is a waste of your time and efforts.

In Breakthrough Action Plan 6, you will learn how to construct a robust budget to help you plan and manage your business financially, giving you confidence that you are in control and can manage your business to produce the profits you desire.

Breakthrough Action Plan 6: Realistic sales forecast and budget

The steps in this plan are all about getting things planned in your spreadsheet software. There is a simple budget template you can download at **www.double-your-business.com**

1 Collect your business bank statements for the past year to help you estimate your budgets for expenses. You can also use them to help estimate sales if you don't track sales in any other way at the moment.

2 Create a spreadsheet (or download the one from the website) with an estimate for each month of the year of how much you will sell and fill these figures in on the sales forecast. When estimating your sales for each month, you can use the following thoughts to help you.

- Certain times of year may be stronger or weaker for your sales performance. Plan for the peaks and troughs with your sales figures – don't simply spread the sales figure evenly across the year.

- When you know that certain periods are always poor, you can plan ahead to either save extra cash, cover costs or do some special promotions to lessen the severity of the slump. If your business is heavily seasonal, this is vital for your company's health.

- Write an action plan to support your increased sales target. Growing your sales requires a clear strategy to make it happen.

3 Put in the cost of goods sold part of the spreadsheet figures to reflect the costs of hitting these sales figures. Only include costs that are incurred directly as a result of the sales.

4 Fill out the total expenses area at the bottom, again using the past history in your bank statements to budget your future spend. If you can determine the precise month that a certain spend has to happen, you can also use your budget to help you reduce the likelihood of cash flow problems around that time.

5 Plan for any major purchases, such as new equipment, vehicles, etc., so that you can see the financial impact on your business.

6 Schedule a regular meeting with yourself each month for 30–60 minutes to review your performance against budget. Answer the following questions during your meeting.

■ Are your sales performing as planned and expected? If not, what can you do about it?

■ Are you sticking within your spending plan, so that net profit is being maintained, or are you losing money by spending too much on your offices?

■ Are you maintaining your gross profit margins, so that you are making as much with every sale as you planned? It's common for salespeople to give a discount to try and make a sale, but sometimes they go too far, so nip this in the bud if you see it becoming too frequent.

■ Have any costs crept up unexpectedly that need to be investigated? It is common to see costs like bank charges, overtime and so on climbing unless they are regularly reviewed and actions taken to keep them under control.

7 If something massive happens in your industry that makes your plans completely wrong, create a new budget for yourself and use it. Don't simply stick to your original plans if it is clearly going wrong; there is no point kidding yourself and it's far more valuable to work from a credible plan than to be frustrated by figures that are a million miles from reality!

Key points from this chapter

■ Strong financial management is a key aspect of business survival and growth.

■ Manage cash flow carefully to avoid running out of money.

■ Pay particular attention to credit control, eliminating old stock as a matter of routine and only drawing as much from the business as it can afford to pay you.

- Establish robust profit margins through strategies that help you introduce higher prices and keep costs down.

- Run your business to a sales forecast and budget to give you a plan for profitable growth.

4

Turn your employees into a gold medal team

The Growth Blueprints for leadership, management and teamworking

Pull a string and it will follow wherever you wish. Push it and it will go nowhere at all.
Dwight D. Eisenhower

Having effective teams is a big part of success in business. At the same time, almost every business has to face people problems at some point – either finding the right quality of employees or dealing with performance and attitude problems. These issues are among the most stressful and tiring to deal with because they are not just logical problems that need to be solved, but involve a walk through the murky area of emotions produced by interpersonal relationships. Knowing how to recruit, lead, manage, develop and retain the right people is a core skill for business growth.

When stressed-out Australian dentist Paddi Lund began hearing voices in his head and seeing visions of dark and unpleasant things, he soon realised that it was his business driving him insane. While taking sedative pills to help him sleep at night, he thought deeply about his work.

He reflected on how he had studied for so long to become a dentist, only to find himself running a business where his customers arrived in pain, didn't appreciate the effort he put into their treatment and complained about paying afterwards.

Inspired by the serene smile on the face of a Down's Syndrome man walking to work, he decided to change the focus of his business to happiness. He called a staff meeting to explain to everybody that the most important thing now was for everybody to feel happy while at the practice – Paddi himself, his team and his customers. The results were profound; Paddi achieved legendary status in dental circles for his unique take on business, as he works fewer hours and earns more, while enjoying an incredibly loyal customer base – more so than any other dentist.

If your business is something you really don't like, read the book he wrote about changing his business from nightmare to dream. It's called *Building the Happiness-Centred Business*.

In this chapter you will discover the essential ingredients to leadership, management and effective teamworking for your own business. Figure 4.1 shows how the three Growth Blueprints covered in this chapter fit together.

At the top, the one-page growth plan provides a basis for communicating the direction and goals of the business, which is the primary focus of leadership. The whole of the drive towards growth in your business is built upon two foundation blocks. It is essential to have these – the *right people* and have them organised and working as *winning teams*.

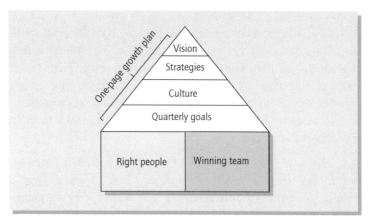

Figure 4.1   A model for leadership, management and a winning team

Growth Blueprint 7: One-page growth plan

Without a clear sense of direction and purpose to your business, work will become a place that you 'attend' every day, without it providing any deep satisfaction of ownership to you.

This Growth Blueprint describes the essential four elements that make up your one-page growth plan – vision, strategies, culture and quarterly goals. With these in place, the practical issues of organising and motivating employees to follow your lead can be confidently addressed later on, using the methods contained in the remaining two Growth Blueprints in this chapter.

Create a powerful vision

When you jump into a taxi, the first thing you do is tell the driver where you want to go. If he doesn't know the place, he'll seek to clarify your destination before he sets off. In fact, if you got into a cab and just told him to go, without a destination, he would probably laugh and tell you to get another ride because without some kind of endpoint, there's no point in moving. Your business is just the same, and by creating a long-term vision for it, you provide a clear direction that can be communicated to your employees, customers and even investors.

Many owners of small businesses would say that their overall business ambition is to reach £1 million or £10 million turnover, depending on their size right now. At least, they would if they were being really candid about themselves. Most of the rest will tell you that they are quite happy as they are, because it's less painful than admitting the truth, which is they have given up trying to grow as they've tried for so long and can't take the knockbacks any more.

The problem with a vision or long-term aim that is based on a turnover figure is that it has no soul – it is a hollow target, a milestone figure that only matters to you. In fact, very few people are motivated by a direct financial goal. Businesses need to have some sense of purpose that goes beyond that. Your vision should be something inspiring for your team. If it is all about making a lot of money for you personally, it is like saying that you are going on a diet and expecting them to make you salads and take you to the gym. They don't have any interest in the results, so it isn't going to happen!

A great example of a long-term vision comes from the *Star Trek* TV and film series: 'to explore strange new worlds, to seek out new life forms and new civilisations, to boldly go where no one has gone before.' This encapsulates a powerful sense of purpose and has become part of popular folklore. Your vision statement's job is to do the same – to provide a real sense of purpose for your business and staff.

How do you create a vision to inspire other people, something that really matters to them? Your business cannot be all things to all people; your job as its leader is to give it direction, set the purpose. One simple way to do this is to decide to be excellent at one particular aspect of it. Paddi Lund decided to create the happiest dental experience around; Domino's Pizza created the fastest pizza delivery service; James Dyson created the bagless vacuum cleaner.

Some people find it easier to choose a big, long-term goal instead of a nebulous, never-ending statement. That's what JFK announced for NASA in 1961, when he said they would, 'send a man to the Moon and bring him safely home again' within the decade. This is different from the *Star Trek* statement because it has a definite end – once a man has been to the Moon and come home safely, the job will have been done. Despite this, it is hugely powerful because it is a very specific goal with a long timescale attached.

Your vision might be slightly scary to you, but, if it's an exciting kind of scary, that's a good thing. So, what would make a compelling vision for your business?

Here are some thoughts to get your creative juices flowing:

■ the most romantic restaurant in London

■ the most luxurious bathrooms for the most discerning customers

■ the nursery that cares most for your child's development.

Each of these sets an aspirational big goal for the business involved. What could your business become, if you let yourself dream?

Identify your strategies for success

If your vision is about the direction, the strategies dictate how you will get there. They are the decisions about where time, focus and money will be invested for growth. An advancing business is one with very clear strategies that rarely change, although they will evolve as progress is made. There will normally be a number of strategies supporting the vision.

Richer Sounds is the UK's largest chain of hi-fi shops, arguably having achieved this position by having a vision of wanting to offer the best hi-fi-buying experience. By looking at its approach, it is possible to identify some of the key strategies that have given the company such a successful competitive advantage. Here they are:

■ open small stores on the outskirts of towns to make them accessible to large populations, while keeping the rent low

- buy end-of-line stock from large manufacturers in bulk, then sell these to customers at big discounts
- keep stock in the store and back rooms to maximise the amount of stock per square metre
- deliver world-class customer service, as evidenced by customer feedback.

Richer Sounds' strategies are easy to understand and their results are inspiring.

Table 4.1 sets out some topics to consider when you brainstorm strategies for your business. These are just prompts to get you started – there will undoubtedly be other things to consider during the development of your strategies.

Table 4.1 Some topics to brainstorm when developing strategies

Technology	Design	Location	Supplier relationships
Business processes	Customer service	Marketing	Stock levels
Terms of business	Quality of materials	Unusual guarantees	Uniqueness
Patents and copyright	Branding	Employees	Colour/size/shape
Opening hours	Home deliveries	Events	Customisation

Whether or not you decide to spend time thinking about strategies, you still have them. For most people running a business, they unwittingly accept the default strategy of being ordinary and largely the same as their competitors! If you really want to double your business, however, you will need to go beyond the ordinary, so take some time to develop your own winning strategies.

To be successful, you need a strategy that delivers or markets your service in some way that your competitors are not doing. Your business does not need to appeal to everybody – just enough people to build a great, loyal customer base. Successful fishing boats do not trawl for every kind of fish; they will specialise in cod or tuna, then become very, very good at maximising their catches. That's your job, too.

> ### Success tip
>
> It is often useful to look outside your industry for ideas that are commonplace in others. For example, one client with an IT repair business introduced a monthly subscription for maintenance, which was inspired by his satellite TV subscription bill.

Define the culture of your business

Among the biggest complaints that business owners make about their employees is that they 'can't do it like I do it', 'they make stupid decisions', 'they just don't seem to understand what's important, even though I have told them so many times before'. Unless they have recruited stupid people, the problem is often that the employees have not been trained to understand the principles on which you base your own decisions.

Designing and sharing these principles is how you define the culture for your business. A strong set of principles identifies the behaviours and values that your business thinks are important. Imagine that your biggest customer, Mr Jones, has a problem and needs a few spare parts in a hurry. Because he is so important to your business, you send them by courier, at your own expense, as a way of looking after him. A week later you are out of the office and another customer has a similar problem. This customer, Mr Green, is one you don't like – he has complained about your prices for years and you really wouldn't care if you lost him. Yet, your team look after him in just the same way as you treated Mr Jones. This costs you £35 in delivery and parts.

Many business owners would blame their staff for being stupid and not knowing that Mr Jones is a good customer, while Mr Green is a bad one, but this is simply a clash of values. Your staff have not been trained to know which customers are Grade A, so have assumed all customers are equal. Following your lead, they would send out a few parts to any customer in this way. That's not what you want at all, yet it's what your staff assumed because you didn't establish principles for working, so they simply copied your behaviour from one random incident. Multiply this story 100 times over with each member of staff and your business begins to run on misplaced beliefs and legendary tales. It's no wonder employees drive some business owners mad!

Defining principles for your business simply means figuring out the rules and making sure that they are clearly understood and enforced. With a written set of principles, new members of staff will quickly understand the boundaries for working there and will become fully effective far more quickly than if they have to learn it all from getting it wrong and being told off first.

Perhaps the most well-known set of principles is the ten commandments in the Bible. They are divided into rules about maintaining religious faith and a moral code. This idea of several different purposes for principles is important in business, too. There will be principles that are important for how customers are treated, principles for teamworking and principles that you would expect from employees. Here is an example of some principles a printing business with a vision to deliver the fastest high-quality print might use.

- **On-time delivery** Our customers choose to use us because they need their print quickly. They are willing to pay a premium for the speed we offer. We take whatever steps we can afford to get their print to them by the time we have promised, even when things go wrong.

- **Quality** Machinery and consumables are bought, maintained and used according to supplier recommendations to ensure customers enjoy the highest quality print available.

- **Respect and enjoyment** We treat each other with respect because it makes working together far more comfortable and enjoyable. We honour our commitments because we understand that respect must continually be earned.

- **Pulling our weight** We take work seriously, putting in the hours and never being idle. When things go wrong, we go the extra mile to get back on track. We take pride in our work and ourselves.

- **Price** We do not try to be the cheapest and we do not offer discounts for one-off jobs. We understand that our value comes from our speed and quality and the customers we have appreciate these factors above all else.

Just these five rules give an immediate sense of how this business would 'feel' if you were to visit it. This is precisely the purpose of creating a culture for your business. Notice how the first two principles – on-time delivery and quality – are all about what each customer wants. Next, there are two principles for how the team behaves – respect and enjoyment and pulling our weight. Finally, there is a principle set by the owner – price.

Set quarterly goals

When the Romans built roads, they would place milestones along the way, showing the distance travelled or distance to a destination city. In the same way, goals can be used as progress markers along the way to achieving your long-term objectives, whether a bold vision or a specific long-term goal. Quarterly goals are recommended because three months is a naturally useful period of time. As well as being the length of a season, it is long enough to achieve visible progress, yet not so long that the sense of urgency can be lost.

A useful acronym when setting goals is SMART, which helps you to check a goal to make sure that it is worthwhile and appropriate. SMART stands for the following.

- **Specific** What exactly should be achieved?

- **Measurable** How will you know the goal has been reached?

- **Achievable** Is it realistic to expect this to be complete by the due date?

- **Relevant** Will doing this actually help to move the business towards the vision?

■ **Time-bound** When is the goal due to be completed?

Setting quarterly goals and reviewing them at team meetings (more of this later in this chapter) creates a sense of urgency and provides accountability for getting things done. Each quarter, the goals are reviewed and new goals set.

Breakthrough Action Plan 7: One-page growth plan

Follow the instructions below to create your one-page growth plan.

1 Write your compelling vision or devise an inspiring long-term goal for your business.

2 Brainstorm your strategies to achieve this vision.

3 Define the principles of culture, remembering to incorporate needs from customers, your team and yourself in these.

4 Set your quarterly goals that start your journey towards the vision.

5 Test that the goals are SMART (see previous page).

6 Create your one-page growth plan using the template at **www.double-your-business.com**

7 At your next team meeting, introduce the plan and get your team involved.

A blank one-page growth plan is shown opposite – you can use this instead of downloading the template, if you prefer to get going right away.

One-page growth plan for _____

Vision	Strategies
	1
	2
	3
	4
	5

Principles of culture	Quarterly goals
	1
	2
• • • • • • •	3

Growth Blueprint 8: Right people

Figure 4.2 shows the building blocks for the 'Right people' Growth Blueprint, but nothing is more important for building an effective team than hiring the right people for the right jobs in the first place. When business owners say that they want to know how to motivate people, it is often because they have hired the wrong people or have put good people into the wrong jobs.

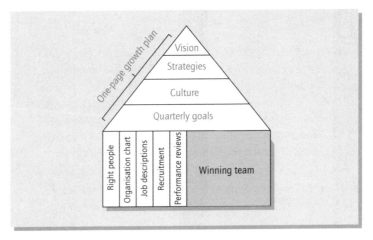

Figure 4.2 The building blocks for the right people

The people you hire are your raw materials. If you let poor-quality people in, you will spend lots of time and energy trying to 'fix' them instead of helping the right people to grow into great performers. At the same time, few people will be motivated for long in a job that does not play to their strengths.

It's difficult to hire the right people every time and it's no fun telling people that they don't fit, either. The result is that business owners try to do everything themselves forever or hire and retain the wrong people, thinking they have to make do with them. This leads to the business getting bogged down and failing to grow. The simple truth is that the longer a problem is allowed to fester, the worse the problem becomes.

This Growth Blueprint solves these fundamental issues in its five elements:

- hiring the right people
- creating an organisation chart to provide a logical structure to your business
- writing job descriptions to clarify who is responsible for what
- recruiting high-performing employees
- running performance reviews with staff to help them grow and develop, while nipping performance issues in the bud.

---

case notes

Stephanie's manufacturing company grew at a very fast rate and the workforce went from 3 to 12. The new employees had been chosen hastily, however, and Stephanie was clocking up 100 hours' work every week. The bulk of this was actually 'covering' for the poor work of some members of staff. One particular person was always late and seemed deliberately slow to finish her work. With outside help, that employee was removed and this immediately lifted the morale of the team.

In her workshop, a new organisation chart and some written job descriptions effectively delegated many decisions from Stephanie to her team. Now, with some free time, she set about recruiting to strengthen her team.

The combination of these actions reduced Stephanie's working week to a far more reasonable 45 hours, also allowing holidays to be taken and weekends to be enjoyed.

The right people

The simplest way to think about great staff is to consider attitude and ability. A perfect organisation will have people who have a great attitude towards working in your business and a strong ability to get the job done. In practice, it's likely that you will have a mix of people from several of the quadrants in Figure 4.3.

Look at the people you currently employ. Consider their attitude and abilities, then mentally categorise them as one of the four types shown in the grid. While the grid is self-explanatory, it is worth stating a couple of key points before going through each of the quadrants in more detail.

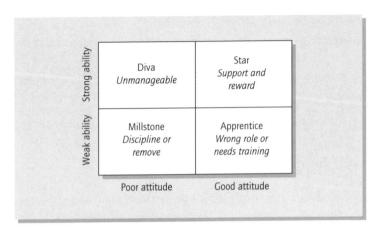

Figure 4.3 Attitude v. ability matrix

Poor attitude doesn't just mean people who are difficult or disruptive but also those people who are somewhat lazy and tend to avoid work.

Ability is all about how good a person is within a particular job. Just like a football team manager would fail if he tried to build a complete team using only strikers, you will need a range of skills in your business. Consider whether or not your employees are in the right jobs to allow them to play to their natural strengths. Simply moving an employee to another job can often be a revelation in terms of the impact this has on productivity.

Millstones

These people have a poor attitude and weak skills. They will drain you of money if you train them because they will not take their training seriously and will not perform well afterwards. If they are unwilling to quickly change their attitude, they will be a bad influence on the rest of your employees and simply pull everybody down. A quick decision to call in professional HR support and help the millstone leave your business with dignity is commonly the best thing you can do.

Apprentices

Apprentices have a great attitude but not the skills to do the job that's required of them. This may be because they are in the wrong job – something that does not play to their strengths – or it may be that they need training and development in order to become fully productive. Thanks to their positive attitude, though, unlike millstones, spending time and money on their training will be a worthwhile investment.

Divas

While they are normally very skilled, divas come with all sorts of baggage in terms of their attitude. They may be a little lazy or may be simply difficult and argumentative. Managing these people is very difficult and can take extraordinary patience, but they can be productive and important to your business because of their skills. That's why the diagram calls them unmanageable. If you do want to try and change them, consider getting some professional help to guide you. You will have to make a decision with each diva in your organisation, depending upon the value they bring versus the total cost (time, money and stress) of employing them.

Stars

Terrific employees, stars perform at a very high level and are a joy to work with, due to their skills and attitude being a strong match for the jobs that they do. It's important to look after your stars and make sure you provide them with the support they need to work well and reward them appropriately. If a star feels that he or she has been neglected by the boss, after a while your star will simply choose to move to another business in the hope of being better appreciated.

Experience suggests that, in a business with ten people, there will be at least one millstone, three to five stars and the rest will be made up from a mixture of apprentices and divas. The single most valuable thing to take from this Growth Blueprint is that your best employees will all quietly applaud the removal of millstones, yet most would never have taken action to bring this about themselves. This one thing will make a profound improvement to your business.

Your challenge – as the owner of a business – is to recruit the right people and train them all to move towards the star quadrant. A good practice for the future health of your business is to consider the potential for future development when recruiting new staff. It makes sense to recruit at least a few staff with the potential to move up one or two levels, so that, as your business grows, they will grow with it, stay motivated and support you.

Ask yourself whether or not your small business can thrive with problem employees. My thoughts on poor performers may seem harsh, but in a small business you focus so heavily on these people that they become a massive, unnecessary burden on the rest of the team. Better to talk straight on this topic and deal with the issues head on than pretend that there's no such thing as a poor performer and it's entirely your fault as the manager. There is little joy in working with staff with a poor attitude; enthusiastic, capable staff will make all the difference in the world.

Success tip

When you have staff working for you, there's a tendency to think of them as friends. These are people you employ, however, and they will never think of you as a friend, only as the boss. You can never confide any deep concerns or worries to any employee. Be fair, honest and firm with them if you expect to earn their respect and commitment to work hard for you.

Drawing an organisation chart

An organisation chart is a diagram that shows the different job titles in your business, with you (or your general manager) at the top and your staff arranged below in a clear hierarchy. For each job in your business there needs to be a box.

Figure 4.4 shows a generic organisation chart. A chart like this clearly shows how people are meant to work together in teams and who works for whom. In this example, two salespeople work for a sales manager, the production specialists and quality controller work together as a team for the operations manager and the credit controller works for the accounts manager. The

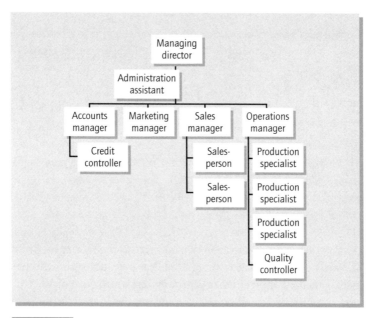

Figure 4.4   Example of an organisation chart

managing director has five people working directly for him or her: the administration assistant, the accounts manager, marketing manager, sales manager and operations manager.

For a small business without staff or very few, drawing an organisation chart for the first time can be a revelation as it provides an opportunity to imagine how the business could be with extra support. The growth of many small businesses is held back by a lack of people. Knowing what jobs your business needs done and taking the time to recruit people to do them can dramatically increase the growth of a business, provided there is adequate finance in place to support it.

If your team has grown gradually over time, you may find that several people share some of the jobs. Drawing the organisation chart is an opportunity to clarify these situations and simplify the way that your business runs by giving each job to just one person.

> ### Success tip
>
> As you draw an organisation chart for your own business, consider how the business needs to look, not necessarily how it is operating right now. When you have created your chart, go through and add the names of the people who currently do each of the jobs. It may be that some people are doing several jobs. That doesn't matter as long as you know who is doing what. If you find that some people have too much to do, an organisation chart helps by both revealing the issue and providing a structure for improvements.

Write job descriptions

As your business grows and you recruit more staff, it becomes increasingly important to make sure that everybody knows what is expected of them. Job descriptions are the key tool for this purpose, used to describe the responsibilities and key measures for each job. They can also be used to help you work through the skills and behaviours required of the people in each position.

A job description is typically one or two pages long and sets out the responsibilities of the job and the qualities of the ideal candidate.

Here is a list of sections to include in your job descriptions:

- **job title** this is the job name that will be used on company stationery, such as business cards or in e-mail signatures
- **location** whether or not the job is based at a specific location, travel is required between locations and if the person can work from home
- **job purpose** one or two sentences summarising why this job exists
- **organisation** where the job fits in the organisation chart – who their manager is, who works for them, etc.
- **key responsibilities** the top 10–15 areas of responsibility of the job
- **key metrics** how the performance of the person in this job will be measured

■ **person description** describes the qualifications (including academic, vocational and others, like driving licence), skills, specific experience and any other attributes of an ideal candidate in this job. Include points relating to attitude here, too, to make sure you get people who will be a cultural fit with your business.

Every great business will have a range of people with very different skills and behaviours. Indeed, if everybody was the same, things would fail because no one person would encompass everything that needs to be done – not even you can be perfect at everything!

Consider a Formula 1 motor racing team. The drivers are a model of controlled aggression, fighting to get past each other and continually taking risks at dangerously high speeds. Meanwhile, the technical team members will be very different characters indeed. They will display incredible patience, attention to detail and creative thinking skills to design cars with an edge over the competition. A racing driver would make a very poor car designer and vice versa. When developing job descriptions, consider the specific traits needed, such as these, and you will have a much greater likelihood of hiring stars for every position.

Recruit high-performing employees

There is a simple mantra to follow when recruiting: hire slow and fire fast. When you rush to fill a job in your team, you invariably see too few candidates, interview them without any real depth and hire them with the hope that they will work out. The following steps describe a far more effective method you can follow to get high-performing people.

Cast your net wide

Use all avenues to advertise your job. Good people tend to know other good people, so ask your best employees and friends to recommend people; use recruitment agencies, online job websites, newspaper adverts, jobcentres, local shop windows, whatever it takes.

Test for skills

Conduct aptitude tests to confirm that candidates have the technical skills you need. This will quickly narrow the field to a few candidates who shine above the rest. It is possible to find technical tests for many disciplines online now or you could ask a recruitment agency to use them with each candidate.

Success tip

Don't judge a book by its cover when recruiting. Here is an unusual true story of the power of aptitude tests.

A degree-qualified mechanical engineer failed an aptitude test, while an unqualified housewife passed the same test. The housewife was recruited to do a production maintenance job and was a great choice. Qualifications and experience are not the same as aptitude or ability!

Review CVs for insights into candidates' histories. Look through the forms from each applicant. Look for attention to detail and pride in his or her work. For example, are the CVs or covering letters full of spelling mistakes? Are there unexplained gaps in their employment histories? Do they stay in jobs or do they jump from place to place? Try to read between the lines to gain an understanding of them from what they tell you.

Interview for attitude and ability

Use the specific behaviours you are after from the job description. In your interviews, ask candidates to give you examples from their real-life situations where they can demonstrate the skills you need in the job. Past performance is the best indicator of future behaviour, so using examples drawn from their actual experience is far better than asking them to explain how they would behave in an imaginary scenario. For example, here is a sequence of questions that might be used to prompt a computer programmer to reveal his or her technical ability.

■ What is the most complex technical situation you can remember having to face?

- What was your goal? What did you need to try to achieve?
- How did you approach this challenge? What specific actions did you take?
- What was the result? How did it go?

You can see how these questions are designed to delve into the past of the candidate and not simply discuss hypotheticals. Also notice that all these questions are open-ended, prompting a detailed response, rather than the simple yes or no you could get by asking a closed question.

The purpose of a good interview is to probe deeper than the CV and find out as much as you can about the character and skills of the candidate. For each aspect of ability and attitude that matters for a job, ask questions of the candidates to uncover how well they performed in similar situations in their past. This will give you a better picture of their value than asking them what they would do in a fictitious situation.

Try them for a day

Invite your top candidates in for a day to try the job out for size. This gives you and them the chance to see how they would fit in with your business. This won't work for all jobs, but, wherever possible, it can be a very fast and effective final step of interview. You then pick the best one for the job.

Fire fast!

If the candidate does not work out, you will sense it very quickly. Listen to your instincts and deal with it as soon as you can.

Success tip

Most small businesses don't follow up references – make sure that you do. Ask candidates to supply the contact details of three referees. When you ring those people, they may be reluctant to be completely candid if the person was a poor performer. By describing the job they have applied for, however, you can ask if they would be likely to thrive in that kind of environment.

You can also ask them, 'Oh, just one more thing, completely off the record – knowing what you do about them, would you take this person on again?' All you need is a simple 'yes' or 'no' answer.

Hold regular performance reviews

The job descriptions form the basis for understanding how well somebody is performing at work. A performance review meeting is where you sit down with each employee individually to see how they are doing.

While most business owners don't do this at all, those who do mostly only manage to do it once each year. This is fine for more senior employees who are already stars, but, for anybody who is still developing and improving their performance, a more regular review provides an ideal opportunity for you to give them feedback on how they are doing, along with some advice and support to help them improve. Monthly or quarterly can be good intervals for reviews with staff you are actively developing. A simple procedure for performance reviews is described in the following Breakthrough Action Plan.

Breakthrough Action Plan 8: Right people

Follow these actions to take a big first step towards improving your people management skills.

1 Draw an organisation chart:

- include a box for each job in the business.

- add in the names of the people currently doing the jobs.

- eliminate any overlap, where two people are sharing the same job.

2 Review the people in your business, using attitude and ability as your key filters.

- Your millstones need to be moved to become productive or removed altogether. Mentally decide who they are and write down half a dozen situations for each one that explains why they are a problem. Then consult an HR specialist to work out the next steps.

◼ Identify employees who fit into the apprentice quadrant. If they have skills that are not being used, move them into a job that plays to their strengths. Otherwise, design a training plan for them to lift their technical skills, allowing them to move towards the star quadrant.

◼ Identify your divas and consider whether there would be sufficient value to be gained from a training plan to change their attitude. Sometimes it's better to just leave them to get on with their technical work – changing someone's attitude is far harder than teaching them a technical skill.

3 Develop job descriptions for every job in the business. Download a template from **www.double-your-business.com**

4 Identify the gaps in your organisation, places where additional staff would improve profitability and/or cash flow. Recruit to fill these gaps using the recruitment method described earlier.

5 Schedule regular performance reviews for each member of staff. Use these steps as a starting point:

◼ Provide each employee with a copy of his or her job description.

◼ Ask the employees to nominate several colleagues to provide feedback on their performance.

◼ Ask the employees how they think they performed against their job descriptions.

◼ Gather facts and figures to include in your review meeting – these will typically be the performance metrics given in the job descriptions.

◼ Hold the reviews in a private room. Go through all of the above points and discuss how they are doing. Praise high performance and agree training, where appropriate, to help people to improve.

◼ Set a date for your next review meeting.

Growth Blueprint 9: Build a winning team

Teamworking brings together elements from leadership and management. A great team can only exist within the context of good leadership, which means it's important to sort out your one-page growth plan and deal with any people issues before moving on to the 'winning team' part of the model for leadership, management and a winning team shown in Figure 4.1 at the beginning of this chapter.

There is a great deal more to building a winning team than simply putting together a group of talented people and hoping that they will automatically achieve high performance. In fact, one only needs to look at the performance of national sports teams to realise that the best groups of players do not always produce the best results when they cannot gel together effectively.

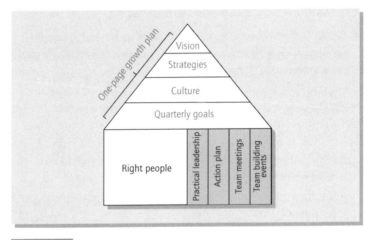

Figure 4.5 The elements that make winning teams

In this Growth Blueprint you will learn how to improve the performance and output of the people in your business by getting them to operate more effectively as a team. Figure 4.5 shows the four elements of teamworking:

- practical leadership
- an action plan
- team meetings
- team building events

Getting your team to work is about spending time with them to inspire them with the vision, reinforce the culture and hold them accountable to an action plan. Over time, the team meetings and team building will improve communication and improve working relationships between team members.

Practical leadership

Leadership happens at many levels in a business. The overall vision and direction of the business, the culture and goals are all created with what might be termed *strategic leadership* – meaning that it is done once and then largely left alone. On a day-to-day basis, however, more practical leadership is needed to bring those ideals to life and generate and maintain momentum and spirit within the team.

Practical leadership is something that occurs in many different ways and is often shown by members of staff, not just the business owner. For example, when a customer has a serious issue and the business owner is unavailable, the person who steps up to the plate to deal with the situation professionally is showing practical leadership. It is essential, as the business grows, to nurture and grow the leaders within your team to be more capable of taking the reins when you are busy elsewhere (or on holiday).

The simplest guidance for practical leadership is to identify the key behaviours expected. These then become your personal standards of behaviour as the business owner.

- **Results focus** There must be a relentless focus on getting things done, from the top down. As the business owner, make sure your actions get done on time to lead the way. Hold everybody else accountable to also get their actions done on time.
- **Role model of culture** For your team to believe in the principles of culture for your business, first and foremost you must be seen to live by and uphold them. You cannot stand by when a principle is ignored; it must be immediately confronted if the culture is to be more than just words on paper.
- **Steady guiding hand** When things go wrong and drastic action is needed to regain control, employees sometimes lose their heads and go to pieces. Practical leadership dictates that they will look to you for direction, reassurance

and instruction. Learn to think calmly under pressure so that you are solid as a rock for your staff.

- **Inspire with your vision** At every opportunity, remind your team what your business stands for and where it is going. The vision must be brought to life through your words and actions, inspiring your team to believe in it as much as you do.

- **Guardian of standards** Shoddy work must not be allowed to slip through. As the leader of the business, set clear guidelines for every important detail and act as the final arbiter of whether work is good enough or not. Never let standards slip.

- **Engage and involve** A fully effective team is one in which everybody feels part of something worth working towards (engagement) and everybody is contributing and participating (involvement). Practical leadership actively works to engage and involve everybody in the business; nobody should feel left out.

- **Build trust** The most successful teams have incredibly high levels of trust between members; they simply know that they can depend upon one another. Constantly look to develop team members to help them inspire trust in themselves. The stronger the bonds of trust in your team, the more highly it will perform.

An action plan

The action plan is your 'secret weapon' for getting your team to take charge of any changes that need making to improve the business and to make them happen quickly. It is really a component of team meetings, but it is so important to success that it is given its own section. Many people in business think that *they* have to do all the things to change or improve their business, but the action plan engages your team, too, which is a much smarter way of working.

During team meetings, ideas that members of the team offer to improve the business are captured on a flipchart and turned into actions. They are then asked to volunteer to do the actions and are assigned to them. Finally, the individuals agree when they will be done.

A vital part of successfully using an action plan is getting your team to come up with most of the ideas, take on the actions themselves and set their own deadlines for getting things done. People become far more accountable when they have come up with the ideas themselves, taken responsibility for the action and set a date for when it will be done.

Figure 4.6 shows an example of a simple action plan created during a restaurant's team meeting. It shows the actions, who is responsible and when they have agreed to do it.

Action plan		
What?	Who?	Due?
Choose and order new tunics	Jenny	23 Mar
Set up rota for hourly toilet check and clean	Paul	1 Apr
Introduce members-only 'dish of the month'	Chef	1 Apr
Use checklists to make sure we never run out of essential ingredients	Chef	10 Mar
Use forms to gather names, e-mails and birthdays	Stuart	23 Mar
Start weekly e-mails to encourage repeat customers	Stuart	1 Apr
Always ask customers if they would like coffee or tea after their meal	Jenny	10 Mar

Figure 4.6   Action plan produced during a restaurant's team meeting

This action plan is typical of the kinds of things that might come out of a good team meeting. What you are after is something similar for your business, with some quick wins that make an immediate difference (here there are tunics, checklists and offering tea and coffee), with some longer-term actions that will take a while to deliver benefits (like the 'dish of the month' and weekly e-mails).

The more that your team can see the changes happening, the

more they will believe in you. The big secret to motivating your team with these meetings is *momentum*. It is imperative that, once you get things moving, you keep driving your team and the actions along at a rapid pace. That is the value of your regular team meetings.

> ### Success tip
>
> Graphs are a great way to track progress and can be used in team meetings to show improvements far better than showing numbers or just talking it through. Make the effort to use graphs and always design them so that, when things get better, the graph moves upwards or upwards and to the right.

Team meetings

On a monthly or even weekly basis, depending upon the number and scale of tasks you are tracking, a meeting to review progress on actions and remind the team of what you are working towards will keep your vision and strategies alive.

Here are two agendas to consider using in these team meetings. The first is the usual meeting agenda and the second is a special case – the launch meeting – which is useful to get the ball rolling with your growth programme.

Team meeting agenda

1   **Open the meeting**

    At the start of the meeting, check that everybody is present and take a moment to remind them of the importance of their contributions towards the vision.

2   **Review actions from previous meeting**

    Make sure things have been done by running through the action plan and asking for an update on the status of each task from the person who volunteered to do it. If something has not been done, ask questions to find out what went wrong and offer help to resolve it. Finally, reschedule the action and review it again the following month.

3 **Progress metrics review**

As well as the individual actions, what do the numbers say about progress? A growing business with a high-performance team would expect to see numbers improving from meeting to meeting, generating a buzz and contributing to a feeling of success.

4 **Issues and help needed**

Sometimes problems arise that cannot be solved immediately by the person responsible. A good team will offer help and it's important as you grow your team to provide a space where issues like this can be raised.

5 **Ideas**

Each meeting may provide one or two further ideas for growth, if you create space for it in this way.

6 **Action plan**

Update the action plan as per the launch meeting below, with names and dates against each action.

7 **Agree next meeting date**

Launch meeting agenda

At the start of any project – including a decision to change the way that you work with your team – the team needs to understand what is going on. A proven way to do this is via a launch meeting to engage your team with the vision, introduce the strategies and discuss the culture. As a shared event for the team, it also provides something that they have in common for them to talk about. Because it is a one-of-a-kind sort of meeting, here is a suggested agenda.

1 **Explain the reason for holding the meeting**

You are changing the way the business works and you need your team's help to make it more successful and a more rewarding and enjoyable place to work.

2 **Tell the story of the business up to this point in time**

Explain what is good and what is not so good and invite comments from the team. Take note that constructive feedback is the idea here, rather than opening up old wounds. While a little honesty about the past or current situation is fine, the mood must not become negative – the meeting must maintain a positive and forward-looking perspective.

3 **Introduce and reinforce the vision**

Even if they already know the vision for the business, tell it to them again. Explain why it matters and how it will make a difference to other people. If the business' vision is really not something that your staff can be directly excited about, consider pledging a sum to a charity that they choose for hitting certain targets.

4 **Define progress metrics**

While working on a long-term target, it is important to know how far you have gone towards reaching it. This is what progress metrics are for. For a Formula 1 driver, racing around a track, it would be laps completed and his position on the leader board. For a business, it might be the number of new customers gained in the previous month, level of customer attrition, total number of orders, etc.

5 **Brainstorm ideas for growth**

The more ideas your team provides, the more engaged they will become. Write a list of all the ideas your team generates, no matter how crazy – idea generation should be fun.

6 **Action plan**

Create your action plan by filtering, with your team, the best or most practical ideas and write them down. Ask for volunteers to take responsibility for actions and agree with them dates for completion.

7 **Create your rules**

What are the rules your team members need to follow to work well? Get their suggestions and let them help you define the limits of behaviours. If they make up the rules, they will be unable to complain when they are enforced!

8 **Agree next meeting date**

Before you finish, plan another meeting so that your team knows the actions will be followed up.

Team building events

The purpose of a team building event is to help develop more trust between members by helping them to get to know each other better.

In a typical team, there will be a mixture of outgoing and reserved people with different interests. When these people are brought together without knowing each other at all, there may be friction simply because they are different from each other. Getting the team members to know and like each other on a deeper level, in a safe environment, can help to build a far stronger feeling of belonging together. This can be done in a number of ways, both with and without external help.

A powerful activity to include in your team building events is some form of simple personality test, to help your people to understand their own behaviours and those of their colleagues, too. With an experienced consultant to lead the process, it helps to build trust and understanding of one another, making working together more fun, simply because it's good to know what makes people tick. Focus on strengths in these sessions to build self-esteem and positivity in the team. If there are weaknesses identified that need to be addressed, deal with these in private individually with the employees concerned.

Using an outside facilitator is really important with team building events because they take the weight off your shoulders in terms of content and getting everybody to participate. Having somebody else running it allows you to enjoy being a part of the experience with your team, ensuring that you get the most out of your investment in the event.

Success tip

A team grows stronger through sharing experiences. Celebrating together can create some *fun* shared experiences.

The perfect reason for a celebration is achieving some great results, but don't ignore seasonal opportunities, like Christmas parties, birthdays, bonfire night, summer barbeques, etc. Keep it informal and, most importantly, have fun. As time passes, you will notice how some events become a part of your team's folklore. These will build strong bonds between team members.

Breakthrough Action Plan 9: Build a winning team

Follow these steps to turn your employees into a motivated, committed and highly-performing team.

1 Look at the model in Figure 4.5 again and make a note of any weaknesses you may have. In particular, take action so that you have:

■ a clearly stated, motivating vision for your business and team

■ the right people doing the right jobs.

2 Run your launch meeting.

■ Consider using a facilitator to help you plan and get the most value out of your event.

■ Book a suitable venue for the meeting.

■ Inform the team of the date of the meeting.

■ Hold the meeting and let your team members contribute significantly to the production of the action plan.

■ Write up the action plan and let everybody have a copy.

■ Write up the rules and let everybody have a copy.

3 Schedule your performance review meetings. These should be at least monthly, if not fortnightly or even weekly if you plan to get things done fast.

4 Hold a team building event. Again, consider using a facilitator for this.

5 Book some celebrations into the diary! Find excuses to celebrate something at least twice each year.

Key points from this chapter

■ Having a compelling vision, supported by clear strategies, culture and quarterly goals, will go a long way towards engaging your employees and achieving growth.

■ There is never any substitute for having the right people in the right jobs in your business.

■ Regular team meetings build momentum and ensure effective communication.

■ You are the leader and the employees will expect you to lead the business forwards.

5

The double your business marketing plan

The Growth Blueprints for massive lead generation

On the average, five times as many people read the headline as read the body copy. When you have written your headline, you have spent eighty cents out of your dollar.

David Ogilvy

The *Double your business* definition of marketing is generating leads for your business from new and existing customers. For your business to have a faster rate of growth will almost certainly require more leads for your salespeople to convert into customers, yet marketing is surrounded by greater misunderstanding, more untruths and unreliable myths than any other aspect of business. It makes the task of promoting a small business an expensive game of trial and error, without any clear guidance about what works and what does not.

It is easy to be misled into believing that the key to good marketing is to follow clichés like, 'You need to get your name out there', 'Let people know you are here' and 'You must have a website', yet none of these will matter if done independently of a master plan to tie them all together for effective lead generation.

This chapter presents five Growth Blueprints that form the backbone of a highly effective marketing plan – one which has already powered the growth of many small businesses.

When companies create an effective marketing plan and manage it ruthlessly, their progress can be meteoric, yet some 80 per cent of businesses fail to grasp the importance of building a plan, relying instead on word of mouth and random good luck to fill their future business pipelines. This chapter provides you with the tools to build a marketing strategy to drive growth. It also explains why you need to get several things right before any of it will work.

Some of the ideas in this chapter will not be new to you. It is likely that you will have tried at least some of them, but perhaps not achieved the results you expected. Unfortunately, that is how marketing plays with you – rewarding efforts with frustration and delight in equal measure. I would urge you to read those ideas with fresh eyes and perhaps consider, if tried again, the ideas might work when done a little differently.

The *sequence* of Growth Blueprints in this chapter provide the marketing plan – take them out of sequence and they will be unlikely to produce the results you desire; do them in order and you just may be pleasantly surprised at the results.

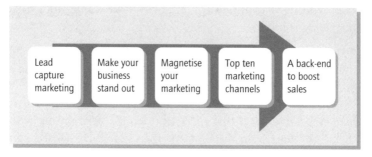

Figure 5.1 The double your business marketing plan

The Growth Blueprints needed to construct your marketing plan are shown in Figure 5.1. Although each Growth Blueprint *can* stand alone and will improve the marketing of your business substantially, it is only when all are working *together* that it will behave as a lead-generating machine, capable of producing leads automatically.

Growth Blueprint 10: Lead capture marketing

Marketing has one purpose for the small business: to generate leads and enquiries that will result in sales. The challenge is to do this efficiently, which is what this chapter is designed to achieve. There are two hurdles to overcome.

- Most attempts at marketing by small businesses simply don't work. The value of sales generated by typical attempts to advertise generate far less business than they cost. Measuring your marketing will quickly help you to cut out marketing efforts that do not work.

- People rarely buy the first time they see an advert, visit a website or walk into a shop. They are browsing or researching. To be in with a chance of selling to these people, create a marketing loop, which will help you keep in touch with them until they *are* ready to buy.

Measure your marketing

To eliminate marketing that does not produce leads economically, you need to measure how many leads come from each marketing strategy.

People are either researching or buying, but it is important to note that, typically, fewer than 5 per cent actually buy during a first visit to a website or a first walk through a shop. They buy when they are *ready* to buy and not a moment before. Smart marketers understand this and seek to build a relationship with their customers from the moment they start their research. To do this, capture some information at the earliest possible opportunity so that it is possible to keep in touch with them after they leave. At a bare minimum, obtain their name and a contact method – ideally, a valid e-mail address.

Success tip

If you have three different marketing methods, make sure you know which leads are coming from which method. You could use a unique phone number for each one and count the number of times each number rings to compare the methods. Another clever way is to use a coupon or offer code for an advert.

case notes

Edward wanted to get more customers for his small car repair business. He was running ads on local radio, in local newspapers and had done a leaflet drop. To identify which of these was producing his leads, I drew up a simple tally sheet for him (see Table 5.1). He started to ask new customers how they found him and, after a few weeks, he had captured this useful data.

Table 5.1 Tally sheet to count number of leads generated by each marketing channel

Advert	Number of leads	Number of sales
Daily newspaper ad	JHf JHf JHf JHf III	JHf II
Local radio ad	IIII	
Leaflet	JHf JHf JHf JHf JHf JHf	JHf JHf I
Word of mouth	JHf	III

The data were transferred from the tally sheet to a table that correlated the cost of each marketing strategy with the number of leads and new customers produced (see Table 5.2). Here is how it looked (rounded to nearest £1 for simplicity).

Table 5.2 The return on investment for different marketing channels

Advert	Cost of campaign	Number of leads	Number of sales	Cost per lead (campaign cost/number of leads)	Cost per new customer (campaign cost/number of sales)
Daily newspaper ad	£500	23	7	£22	£71
Local radio ad	£4000	4	0	£1000	n/a
Leaflet	£450	30	11	£15	£41
Word of mouth	£0	5	3	£0	£0

From Table 5.2, it is clear that word of mouth marketing performs best, as the leads it produces are free and convert easily into customers. It can only produce a trickle of leads, however, and they are unpredictable, depending upon who happens to be talking about your business and when.

Of the commercial marketing channels, the leaflet campaign produced customers for £41 each, so Edward could expand his leaflet distribution campaigns to generate more leads. The newspaper ads might work better if a different ad was tried. Finally, the radio ad was just so far off profitable that it should be dropped.

Note the cost per new customer figures are used to compare different marketing strategies. These are very useful figures that can help you to decide where to invest in advertising and where to cut back. Figure 5.2 shows how these figures are calculated.

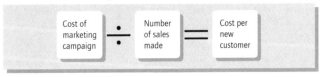

Figure 5.2 How to calculate the cost of advertising per new customer

Money spent on marketing can be wasted when you are not measuring the results. It is like shooting arrows – you will never know if you are shooting in the right direction unless you set up a target and check to see if your arrows are hitting it! Understanding the cost per new customer formula will transform your marketing from wishful thinking into an investment in growth. When new customers can be bought for a known cost, growth becomes far more predictable.

Success tip

Savvy business owners look at the overall *lifetime value* of customers, not just the value of the first sale. Think about this: does your dentist treat a school leaver as a visitor who is worth just £60 for a check-up? Imagine if the dentist thought about the potential of every school leaver to refer his or her future children, while needing more extensive treatment personally in later life. Perhaps the lifetime value of that lead is £10,000 or more.

Introduce a marketing loop

A marketing loop is how a business keeps in touch with leads until they are ready to buy. Most small businesses are not familiar with this idea, so are losing half or more of their potential leads (and sales) because they fail to keep in touch with people who are not yet ready to buy. According to a client in the travel industry, online customers make their purchases after an average of 50 searches. Retailers describe how customers browse through their shops and don't buy anything. Restaurants complain that many customers come once and are never seen again, despite appearing to enjoy their meals.

Everyone who walks past your business, walks through it, passively scans your ads in the paper or sees the sign on your car is a potential new customer for you. Make them stop and give you their contact details, then you can keep in touch with them until they are ready to buy. The same is true for one-time customers. Your marketing loop is the method you can use to keep in touch with them going forwards.

There are two parts to the marketing loop: data capture and follow-up.

Data capture

Data capture is where contact information is obtained and this becomes a lead for your business. The minimum information to capture is a name and e-mail address, because with these it's possible to keep in touch with a personalised e-mail on a regular basis. Another option is to capture either a mobile phone number, so you can use SMS messages, or direct mail letters.

E-mail is the favoured approach for most businesses because the cost of sending e-mails is so small, but using direct mail occasionally can help most businesses. For certain types of business, such as restaurants or a paintball business, weaving SMS messages into the mix can be used to generate an immediate response from your marketing loop. There is a great example of using SMS in the Riverside Restaurant story in Chapter 9.

The most successful method for obtaining contact details is to offer something of value to the customer or enquirer. Typically this will be a free report or guide, if it's from your website, or a chance to win a prize in a monthly draw, if it's a bricks and mortar business. The key point with data capture is to utilise it wherever new leads can be found: cold-calling on the telephone, trade shows and exhibitions, networking events and so on.

Note that there are laws relating to unsolicited e-mails, so be sure to follow guidelines for obtaining permission. One approach is to follow up with an initial e-mail that asks them to click a link to confirm that it's OK to send them e-mails.

Follow-up

Follow-up keeps in touch with new leads to nurture them and build familiarity.

An automated e-mail system called an auto-responder is a powerful and affordable way to keep in touch with your customers. An auto-responder can be used to either send a broadcast message

– when you write and send something immediately – or a prewritten series of e-mail messages at predetermined intervals over a period of weeks and months. Each e-mail can be automatically personalised with the name of the recipient, which helps to create a sense of personal contact and increases the effectiveness of the mailing.

It is worth keeping in touch with people forever because you never know how long it will take them to buy. I have sold to people who have been on my mailing list for four years. Finally, they were ready to work with me. It costs you nothing and, while they can unsubscribe if they want to stop hearing from you, if you offer them something useful, they will be happy to receive them, even if they are yet to buy from you.

Continuing to keep in touch with people forever via e-mail will push sales up well beyond your expectations. You will be amazed how many people will get in touch after being on your list for months and years – sales you are missing now if you don't do this. In fact, I called it the marketing loop because a loop has no end, which is precisely what your marketing should have.

Success tip

An e-mail is not spam if the reader has agreed to receive it – according to the law. In the eyes of receivers, it is not spam if it contains something that is relevant and interesting to them. A shop selling woodworking tools to hobbyists and professionals that sends out an e-mail each week with tips and special offers is unlikely to offend any of its targeted readers. Tips on how to get a razor sharp edge to chisels will also be relevant and interesting to people in this market. A constant stream of sales pitches, on the other hand, will result in people unsubscribing and complaining that they are being spammed.

Breakthrough Action Plan 10: Lead capture marketing

Follow these steps to eliminate poor marketing efforts and begin to capture leads.

1 Introduce a method to capture leads at the earliest possible point.

2 Create a tally sheet for your lead generation and monitor which marketing strategies are working in a cost-effective manner for you.

3 Calculate the cost per new customer for each marketing strategy.

4 Cancel any marketing campaigns that are not producing a profit when compared to customer lifetime value. This may mean cancelling all of your marketing spend if nothing is working.

5 Implement an auto-responder service to keep in touch with your leads.

6 Write 12 e-mails of half a page each (around 250–350 words) to be sent to customers and leads over the next 12 months. Include educational or entertaining content that your customers will enjoy and value.

Growth Blueprint 11: Make your business stand out

Being in business means competing with all the other companies from which your customers can choose to buy. The Internet makes it possible for people to search nationally and internationally for alternative places to buy. Now, more than ever, it is imperative to give your customers a clear reason to choose you instead of your competitors. This is called *differentiation* and this Growth Blueprint will show you how to make your business the obvious choice for your customers. If customers are not given a clear differentiator, they will choose based on something that is obvious to them, which is often the lowest price.

To put your business to the front of the queue, it will need to have three elements:

■ niche

■ unique selling point

■ risk reversal guarantee.

While not every business will want or need to have *all* these elements, the one that most often provides the biggest advantage is niche.

Niche – your clearly defined target market

A *niche* in this context is a specific group of customers who share a common need or problem that can be targeted for marketing. When a business decides to focus on a single niche, it can position itself as an expert for that niche and stand out ahead of the competition. If a person with a bad knee has the choice between a general surgeon or a specialist at a knee clinic, the specialist will win every time because he or she is likely to have treated the same problem many times before and will therefore evoke more confidence in the patient. The same is true in almost every sector of business – the specialist will have a significant advantage over all non-specialists. The secret, then, is to choose a niche with very few other specialists and sufficient demand to build a business around it.

Building your business around a niche does not mean poor profits or poor growth. It is quite feasible to grow into the millions with this strategy. Choosing a niche is not a decision to stop doing any other business, either. Ben Lee, a director at Grosvenor Credit Management & Investigations, created a new service for utility companies in the UK and he won ten major clients within six months. The addition of this niche to his business contributed 60 per cent more sales to an already successful business.

Success tip

A good niche for your business will be one for which you can easily identify and reach a group of customers with your marketing. They will share a common need or problem and have the ability and willingness to pay to solve it.

Unique selling point

A unique selling point (USP) gives your customers a clear reason to choose your products and services instead of your competitors'. It gives your business an edge to help you dominate sales to your target customers. Your USP becomes the constant message that demonstrates the indisputable advantage of your products and services.

The majority of your competitors will have no USP in place at all – they will be simply 'me too' operations, copying each other and competing on price. Your success will ultimately be determined by the quality of your USP – are you a business that adds value to your customers' purchases or are you simply a supplier that they could drop without losing anything special?

The best USP will fill a gap in the market, increasing the satisfaction of customers by giving them something more than they can get anywhere else. When Henry Ford first made cars, he famously stated that 'You can have it in any colour, as long as it's black', so when General Motors came into the business, they offered a real choice of colours, so that people could express their own sense of style through the cars they drove.

Your USP is unlikely to appeal to everybody in your market, but that's OK. Your goal is to appeal to a big enough cross-section of customers with your USP so that you can keep growing your business strongly. Not everybody is going to love your business anyway and having a USP that strongly appeals to a profitable (maybe even upmarket) segment of your niche is precisely the way to grow your business without having to compete heavily on price.

Factors including specialising, time, size/weight, choice, delivery, packaging, personalisation and many more can be used as prompts for an effective USP. Table 5.3 shows some examples for a restaurant and an accountancy practice – the secret is to use imagination.

Table 5.3   Examples of USPs

Factor	Restaurant	Accountant
Speciality	Healthy foods that younger children will love to eat	Home-based businesses
Time	Your food is freshly cooked and served to your table in 15 minutes, guaranteed, or it's free	Your accounts are prepared within 21 days of receiving your paperwork or it's free (when you bring your papers in on time)
Size/weight	All you can eat for £12 per head	We process over £10 million in payrolls every month, so yours will be safe with us, too
Choices	Choose from 15 different home-made pastas and 10 delicious sauces	Standard accounts package or entrepreneur support package with online access to accounts and training videos to understand them
Delivery	Delivery included in the price of every takeaway order	We pick up and deliver your accounts paperwork ourselves to keep it safe
Packaging	Kids' meals in a box with a toy inside	Send in your paperwork each month in the bright pink envelopes provided and your books will be updated within ten days
Personalisation	Birthday cake iced with your name available when ordered at the start of your meal	Includes bespoke 'dashboard' for your business with the specific figures needed to maximise your cash flow and profit

Some of these ideas are workable, some might not be. The point is, though, that 15 minutes of brainstorming produced 7 different USP ideas for both a restaurant and an accountancy practice. There would be many others, too, if the table was expanded to include other ideas (technology came to mind during the brainstorming). From this kind of exercise, it's possible to create a completely different kind of offer from possible competitors' that may just appeal to your niche market.

Risk reversal guarantee

The purpose of your guarantee is to *reverse the risk* of buying from you. Many businesses offer a meaningless guarantee, such as 'best service guaranteed'. Such well-meaning statements give no reassurance to the customer whatsoever and will come across as hollow promises.

The purpose of a guarantee is to overcome any sense of doubt or insecurity about a purchase – 'What if it doesn't work properly?' 'What if it doesn't fit?' 'What if it breaks within a few weeks?', etc. Such are the risks that buyers take. When you provide a powerful guarantee, you take away these risks, allowing them to buy in confidence, knowing that, if it goes wrong, they're covered. Essentially, you guarantee that they can't lose out when they buy from you – a powerful statement indeed.

At first glance, you would think that the risk of a strong guarantee is that you will end up losing more than you make from it, but the vast majority of people are not looking to rip you off – they just want to feel confident that they can buy safely from you. That's precisely what your guarantee offers to them. Here is an example of a guarantee for a personal trainer: 'If you don't feel fitter and healthier within 6 weeks of starting your training programme, just ask and you'll receive a 100 per cent refund, no questions asked.'

Success tip

Many business owners worry about the number of claims they will get if they offer a money back guarantee. In practice, most will see very few claims. People just want to have confidence in what they are buying. Apart from offering them confidence in you, another benefit is that many of my clients who introduced a risk reversal guarantee have increased their prices by 10–25 per cent to cover the small number of claims they may get. They have always profited from it.

Breakthrough Action Plan 11: Make your business stand out

To ensure that your business stands out, follow these steps.

1 Identify your niche market.

2 Create your USP by taking the following action:

- make a list of everything that differentiates your service or product from your competitors'

- know why you would buy from your company – identify the best reasons if you had to justify it to yourself

- if there is nothing unique or special in what you are already doing, take a look at the marketplace and find a new angle that is needed, but nobody else is doing

- combine the most important or just the strongest one into your USP, as a single, powerfully worded sentence or set of bullet points.

3 Create your risk reversal guarantee by taking the following steps:

- brainstorm all of the fears, concerns and misgivings that potential customers might have about buying from you or your competitors

- rank the fears/concerns in order of their importance until you have identified the top one or two

- figure out how to eliminate these top fears – you might need to change the way you work in order to deliver on these

- review the statistics for how often these things can go wrong.

4 Craft your guarantee to eliminate your customers' fears. A good starting template for your guarantee is: 'ABC delivers the best available products. If you are not completely satisfied for any reason, please return your purchase within 30 days for a 100 per cent refund.'

Growth Blueprint 12: Magnetise your marketing

The single biggest reason for most advertising failing is that it focuses on the company and the product, rather than the customer. Successful marketers know that they need to 'magnetise' their marketing using advanced copywriting techniques. In this Growth Blueprint, you will learn to magnetise your own marketing by using the AIDA formula (described shortly) and looking at a worked example that shows you how to use it.

Typical ads created by small businesses and used in places such as newspapers, magazines and on leaflets have a format like the one shown in Figure 5.3. It demonstrates several common failings, but the biggest of these is that it is all about the company, not the customer. It is estimated that people see ads and brand names between 3000 and 30,000 times every single day. It is impossible to pay attention to them all, so the mind quickly tunes out anything that is not of obvious and direct interest to you.

Grey, Green & Brown Chartered Accountants

- Annual returns
- Tax advice
- Audits
- Management accounts
- Local, friendly service
- Established since 1993
- Free first meeting

Phone 01234 567890

Figure 5.3 A typical ad placed by a small business that will produce no leads or sales

Introducing AIDA – your copywriting guide

AIDA is a simple acronym to guide you as you write any ad. Each of its letters describes one of the four elements that an advert requires to be effective. Here is how it works.

■ **Attention** make sure your ad grabs the eye of the reader immediately. As the quote at the start of this chapter states, 'five times as many people read the headline as read the body copy'.

- **Interest** engage the reader's interest and draw them into reading the whole thing.

- **Desire** hook into the emotional needs of the reader and make them want to experience what you sell. A famous marketer once wrote that you need to 'sell the sizzle, not the steak' and it is great advice.

- **Action** once you've told them what is on offer, they need to be told what to do next and be encouraged to take action.

Here is how the advert shown in Figure 5.3 can be rewritten using AIDA. First, a clear target market must be selected so that an advert can be produced to catch customers' attention. For this example, it is home-based businesses. The advert needs to be relevant to their wants and needs and address some of the issues they face.

So, an accountant who chooses to specialise in this niche might offer a service that includes monthly tips to help them plan

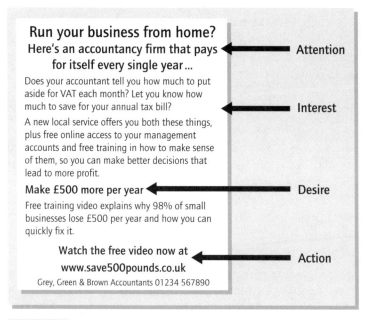

Figure 5.4 Ad constructed using AIDA principles

their taxes better, envelopes to send their receipts and invoices to them in each month, plus an online system to view their accounts and some online videos to teach them a little about their accounts. These things together form a differentiator, giving a strong reason for a small business to choose this accountant rather than another. An advert to sell these facts might look like the one shown in Figure 5.4.

Compare the two adverts in Figures 5.3 and 5.4. AIDA has been used to transform the ad content of Figure 5.3 into something that will draw a home businessperson to read it. While some minor changes may also have to be made in the accountancy practice to provide this differentiation, it means the ad can have a lot of impact.

Here is a run through of how AIDA was used to design this ad.

Attention

The headline 'run your business from home?' will catch the eye of homeworkers because it speaks directly to them. Next, there's a promise that the accountancy firm pays for itself. It is a bold claim that will grab people's attention. The headline only has to grab readers' attention long enough for them to then be drawn in to reading the first sentence.

Interest

When customers start to read the ad, a series of questions about their current accountants will get them interested. It then explains how this accountancy firm offers to teach them how to understand and use their accounts information to make their business better – 'so you can make better decisions that lead to more profit.'

Desire

After attracting their interest, the ad presents an offer of a free video to show them how to easily make an extra £500 profit. It should generate enough curiosity and desire to get leads to take action.

Action

In this case, the call to action is very simple indeed – 'Watch the free video now at www.save500pounds.co.uk.' When potential customers arrive at the site, it will ask for their e-mail addresses and names before showing them the video. These captured leads can then go into the marketing loop, described earlier in this chapter, until they are ready to buy.

Comparing the *before* and *after* versions of the ad, it is clear that people running the first kind of ad would say, 'Advertising doesn't work for me – the only way to get new business in my line of work is through word of mouth.' The truth is quite different: good marketing requires a different way of thinking, but can produce spectacular results when it's done right.

Success tip

To maximise the response to adverts, it is common to try variations of an ad at the same time, but aim them at different recipients. This is known as *split testing* and is a powerful method for helping you to produce the most magnetic marketing. Running the same ad with a different headline, for example, can produce surprisingly different results. If campaigns are large enough, running a split test in the early stages can help to improve the response to them substantially.

Breakthrough Action Plan 12: Magnetise your marketing

To write your own ads that attract clients magnetically, follow these steps.

1 Write down a description of your target market and identify their key needs in relation to your types of products and services.

2 From their key needs, identify several things that your business does that would stand out for those customers.

3 Create an offer that will be attractive to them.

4 Draft your ad using AIDA as a guide:

■ strong headline to grab their **attention**

- hold their **interest** with some key words or facts that you know will be important to them

- build their **desire** by describing how your service or product will make them richer, healthier, happier, more successful, etc.

- make it as easy as possible for the reader to take **action** immediately.

5 Sleep on it. A freshly written ad is rarely the best that you can do – coming back to it a day later will often reveal problems with the first draft and help you to improve it.

6 Test run the ad and measure the response.

7 Repeat the process and continually look to improve the response.

8 Introduce split testing to accelerate the success rate of your ads.

Growth Blueprint 13: Top ten marketing channels

A *marketing channel* is simply a way to get your message to your target audience. While there are hundreds of potential marketing channels, most of your responses will tend to come from a much smaller list.

Looking at what has worked for my clients, here is a list of the ten channels that have most consistently produced the best results:

- direct mail
- lead generation website and pay per click traffic
- networking – online and offline
- referral system
- joint venture marketing
- telemarketing
- signage
- free publicity
- trade shows and exhibitions
- advertising in niche or local magazines, websites and papers.

This doesn't mean that you should abandon any other channels that are working for you, but, in general, these ten will be the most successful.

Direct mail

Direct mail is one of the most powerful marketing techniques available to you, at a remarkably low cost, too. Most people disregard the idea of sending a letter to try and win new business as being old-fashioned or ineffective. Some 'experts' will tell you that it is no longer relevant and you should use some new, technologically advanced marketing techniques, yet direct mail is phenomenally effective when used in combination with your niche and differentiation-based marketing strategy.

The most basic form of direct mail is a letter addressed directly to the person you want to win as a customer. The big strength of direct mail is that you don't waste money hitting every house in a street or every company in the directory. You pinpoint precisely the people you want to target and then carefully craft a letter following the AIDA principles explained earlier.

I have designed direct mail as a strategy with clients selling to both consumers and commercial businesses. One particularly popular technique is to send a postcard, perhaps with a personalised invitation to visit a particular website and view a presentation. Alternatively, you can send a small gift in the post, to make it stand out and really get their attention.

Success tip

My clients have sent out books, toy cars, dolls and even wastepaper baskets, among other things, to make a point with their direct mail campaigns. In one case, three toy cars sent directly to a manager at a major car manufacturer resulted in him picking the phone up that morning and asking for a meeting with my client. This man would not previously even take my client's calls. That is the power of well-designed direct mail.

Lead generation website and pay per click traffic

An incredibly powerful strategy for lead generation for many businesses is to drive visitors to a website using pay per click advertising. Google, Bing, Facebook, LinkedIn and other major online sites provide marketing systems that help you to target people with particular interests. When used with precision it can produce spectacular results. In Figure 5.5 you can see a Google search results page for the search phrase 'Mercedes cars'. The top result on the page, and all the results on the right-hand side of the page, are ads created through Google's Adwords system.

Figure 5.5 Google search results showing pay per click ads at the top and on the right-hand side

If you wanted to target owners of Mercedes cars, you could make an ad appear on this page. Because the ads only cost money when they are clicked, it is called pay per click advertising. It is the most targeted advertising available – it is even possible to make an ad appear only when an *exact* phrase is typed into a search engine. There is a catch to advertising using these systems, however. They are complicated and it is easy to waste a lot of money if you do it without paying attention to the details. There is more advice on how to do pay per click advertising successfully at www.double-your-business.com/ppc

Success tip

One client spent over £10,000 on clicks from its pay per click advertising in a single month without generating a single sale. The firm's website and pay per click account had not been appropriately structured, with the result that clicks had no chance of producing sales. With changes to the website and the account, I helped them to cut their spending to £4000 per month and generate leads that added a staggering £1.5 million sales per annum.

Networking – online and offline

Networking is actively building and nurturing relationships both face to face and online. The true value of networking groups comes from the close relationships that develop between members over time. Strong relationships lead to the regular referral of good-quality business. For example, at one point I was a member of a networking group with an estate agent, property manager, builder and mortgage broker who would regularly pass business to each other, forming a close-knit group that thrived together.

The secret with networking is to think of the relationships in the medium and long term rather than try to make quick gains from them before trust has been created. I saw many characters come along to networking meetings who tried to snipe for business immediately. While one or two managed to pick up a little business, their memberships were short-lived and they did not build positive reputations. On the other hand, those members who consistently contributed and participated over a period of time were the ones who grew and prospered.

For online networking the rules are pretty similar. I have friends and clients who use Twitter, Facebook and LinkedIn groups to generate a proportion of their business. Others use online forums that relate to the niches they have established.

Similar rules apply to both offline and online networking, although there are some sophisticated strategies that you can employ with online networking (especially building your own community) that put you into a position of authority and influence, creating respect for your name within a certain niche.

Success tip

To develop a sophisticated strategy for networking, I recommend *FT Guide to Business Networking*, written by a friend I met through online networking, Heather Townsend. It teaches what Heather calls 'joined-up networking' – linking online and offline together for maximum results.

Referral system

The saying that 'birds of a feather flock together' describes the way that people with particular interests tend to know one another. It's this behaviour that is at the heart of successful referrals. Your best customers will often know others who might also become great customers if you can ensure that you're intro-duced to them.

That's where your referral system comes in. There are three easy types to implement.

■ **Referrer rewards** Offer a reward to existing customers for referrals to new customers. This is very common in the financial services industry, with 'introducer fees' being a lucrative extra stream of income for many people who simply act as middlemen between their own customers and mortgage brokers, loan providers and others. Many banks offer their customers a 'finder's fee' for introducing new customers to them, too.

■ **Shared rewards** A good way to reward referrals is to give the same gift to both the referrer and the person they introduce to you. Cable and satellite TV providers often promote their services by giving the referrer and the new customer they introduce a month's free viewing, or something similar, as a shared reward. That way your customers are rewarded but don't have any feelings of guilt that their friends have paid for their reward as both of them enjoy the same gift.

■ **Relational rewards** Often customers will *want* to give you referrals if they feel that the service you provide is exceptional or where you provide them with something that they would not easily find elsewhere. I call these relational referrals because people are often only too pleased to make the introduction for you, as long as you ask. When you get a referral this way, send a nice 'thank you' card or, perhaps, a small personal gift.

Success tip

It is often difficult for customers to make an introduction on your behalf. If you sell gadgets and toys, it's easy and fun, but, for the rest of us, it's a far trickier introduction. To change this, give away something of value that makes a referral easy. A solicitor could write a guide, 'How to stay friends with your neighbour and still protect your property', for example. That way your customers are not only helping you but they are also helping out their friends.

Joint venture marketing

The phrase 'joint venture' immediately conjures up the image of big corporations launching new business ventures together, but *joint venture marketing* is the idea of marketing to the customers of another business. At the heart of this strategy is finding other businesses that share the same type of customer base as yours, but are not direct competitors.

> **case notes**
>
> An optician specialising in high-end frames and sunglasses arranged a joint product launch with a local luxury car dealer. The dealer invited his clients and the optician invited hers. The glamorous event resulted in new customers for both the dealer and the optician. Now that's a win–win!

In essence, the joint venture is simply a two-way street for helping out fellow, like-minded business owners. Other ways to use this strategy include sending out coupons or vouchers for each other with invoices or in e-mailed newsletters. The real power of this marketing channel is that it provides rapid exposure to a lot of people directly in the right target market, all for minimal cost.

Telemarketing

Picking up the phone and speaking to potential customers – for both business-to-business and consumer markets – remains a very effective lead generation method. Due to some tele-marketers operating with little regard for the people receiving their calls, there are now laws governing who can be called and people can opt out of telemarketing, but, when done properly, telemarketing remains a fast and effective way to win new business.

If you are comfortable about picking up the phone and calling people to generate leads, it will prove to be one of the most valuable techniques to win new business that you will ever use. If you are not comfortable doing it, but want to use this channel, try to find a good-quality telemarketing firm that will provide you evidence of the key results of their efforts.

Success tip

Many freelance telemarketers like to charge by the day for their work. Always seek to negotiate a price per appointment or lead generated rather than pay a daily rate. This aligns their motivation with yours – generating leads – rather than simply charging for their time.

Signage

Commercial premises and vehicles can become very effective signboards for a business. If allowed by local by-laws, an A-frame-style sandwich board outside of a property can be used to indicate special deals and offers on a daily basis. These are often used by pubs and restaurants, but can also be used by shops. Trades such as joiners, builders, electricians, gardeners and so on can use A-frames outside the properties where they are working to advertise their services.

case notes

A client that specialises in repairing wooden sash windows in older houses around London had a plain white van that would be parked outside customers' houses all day long. The customers generally had older houses and would be in streets full of similar properties. When the firm had a sign painted on the van with big lettering that stated 'Specialists in Traditional Wooden Sash Windows', it produced an extra lead per day for them.

Success tip

The same rules apply to signage as to any ad – use the AIDA guide to encourage people to respond. Too many people just put their company name and phone number on signs and it is such a wasted opportunity.

Free publicity

To get free publicity, remember that journalists want a story, not an ad. Sending them a story that's just a thinly veiled promotion will have no chance of publication. A story with some real interest to the papers' audience will catch the eye of the journalists who receive it. For example, a chiropractor I know could have written a great press release about the prize chicken he treated!

Here are seven story ideas that journalists will love:

- new product launch, especially if it's a bit special or unusual
- something quirky – like the chiropractor treating a chicken
- an achievement, such as breaking a record, celebrating the business' anniversary or winning an award – many clients have won awards and gained free publicity in local papers as a result
- donating time or money to a good cause
- helping the local community in some way
- publishing a white paper or special report on something of interest
- become known as an expert on your niche – journalists will approach you for your opinion.

Consider also which media you'll target. A specialist engineering firm selling to the aerospace industry that manages to get its story into the local paper might feel good, but this will probably not produce any enquiries. On the other hand, the same story submitted to aero industry magazines and papers could generate some real interest from potential customers.

Trade shows and exhibitions

These are often incredibly lucrative events because nearly every visitor is a potential customer.

The secret to getting the maximum value from these events is to collect a business card from every single person who walks past your stand. The easiest way to do this is to have a draw for two bottles of champagne, entered by people dropping their business cards into a box or bowl.

A great tip is to make a quick judgement call the moment you see the job title on a person's card to decide whether to draw them into conversation on your stand immediately.

The secret to success is getting all these names into your marketing loop. Most people will make purchasing decisions after the event, so consistently following up your list of names captured at the event will produce strong sales for months afterwards.

To be successful with these events, consider these key factors.

- **Differentiators** What makes your product stand out from the competition?
- **Signage** How will you attract people to your stand?
- **Lead capture** How can you gather contact information for later?
- **Follow up** What will you include in your follow-up that will be relevant and interesting?

---

case notes

One client firm captures the bulk of its trade at exhibitions. The firm manufactures clothes for a niche that is unique, thanks to the process used. It puts a huge amount of effort into dressing its stand to really catch people's attention and, thanks to its strong differentiation, generates a high volume of leads by exhibiting at just three or four events each year. The firm picks up many trade accounts that order in bulk, making it an easy and lucrative business.

Advertising in niche or local magazines, websites and papers

There are many thousands of specialist publications and websites, which provide very direct channels to a target audience. One client sells cardmaking materials and equipment for the burgeoning home crafts market. It advertises in a whole range of niche magazines and generates substantial sales from each copy. Meanwhile, a mortgage broker found that his ads in a property investment magazine produced lucrative customers, while a restaurant's offer in a popular local newspaper produced a flood of new diners.

Success tip

The secret, as with press releases, is to focus on advertising in the publications that will be read by people who are likely to want to buy what you produce or do. The biggest secret of all marketing is simply to put the right message in front of the right people, which is far smarter than the more usual putting a weak message in front of a wide audience. Advertising in the wrong places almost guarantees failure, while just a little thought can open up a whole new way to find customers.

Breakthrough Action Plan 13: Top ten marketing channels

Follow these steps to choose your marketing channels. Download the marketing channels form at www.double-your-business.com and fill it in on your computer. Alternatively, you can use the form given in Figure 5.6.

1 For each marketing channel, complete the line for the form as follows.

- In the column headed 'Appropriate to niche?', write 'Yes', 'No' or 'Maybe', as appropriate.

- In the column headed 'Sales potential', write a figure that is your best guess for the annual sales available through effectively exploiting the channel.

- In the column headed 'Budget', write how much you would need to invest in that specific marketing channel to produce a worthwhile return.

- In the column headed 'Decision/comments', write your decision regarding whether or not you will be using that marketing channel. It may be helpful to enter your reasons for the decision here, too, in order to discuss it with your support network.

2 After completing the form, decide upon the priority of each chosen marketing channel. Write the priority – starting with 1 for highest – alongside the name of each channel on the form.

3 Write an action plan to put the chosen marketing channel to work.

Figure 5.6 Marketing channels form – use it to evaluate which channel is best for you (download from www.double-your-business.com)

Marketing channel	Appropriate to niche?	Sales potential	Budget	Decision/comments
Direct mail				
Lead generation, website and pay per click traffic				
Networking – online and offline				
Referral system				
Joint venture marketing				
Telemarketing				
Signage				
Free publicity				
Trade shows and exhibitions				
Advertising in niche or local magazines, websites and papers				

Growth Blueprint 14: A back-end to boost sales

It is estimated that winning a *new* customer costs six times more than selling to an *existing* customer, yet most businesses concentrate on generating new sales rather than selling again to customers they have already won at least once. While winning new customers is important, more emphasis needs to be placed on creating a profitable back-end, because sending offers for other products and services to repeat customers can provide a huge flow of extra business.

There's another important aspect to this, which is business resilience. If you sell just a single product and the market for it collapses for some reason (think of beef farmers during the BSE crisis or mortgage brokers when the credit crunch began), your business is immediately in peril. If, instead, you also have another stream of income that is sold to the same customers, it gives your business stability in the event of unforeseen circumstances.

A good example of adding a back-end to sales is demonstrated by central heating firm Superwarm Services. They provide long-term servicing to clients after they have purchased a new boiler, introducing the opportunity to create customers for life (rather than just focusing on boiler replacement) from each new lead they generate.

When you look at the first sale to a customer as the beginning of a relationship with them, it pays to consider what the rest of the relationship will bring in terms of additional sales. There are opportunities to either promote your own goods or offer 'partner promotions' to your customers in return for a percentage of the fee. In the Internet marketing world, this is commonly called *affiliate marketing*. It is similar to joint venture marketing, but affiliate deals include a direct payment of commission, while joint venture marketing is sending their offer to your customers and yours to their customers.

Breakthrough Action Plan 14: A back-end to boost sales

If your business is missing a back-end, here are some steps to help you build one.

1 There may be some extra products or services that you already know about, but have not got around to doing. These are the obvious first place to start to expand your back-end.

2 Brainstorm products and services offered by other businesses that you could partner with.

3 Create a list of new products and services that you can offer.

■ Make sure there is a clear connection between what customers have bought and what you are offering. A butcher stocking recipe cards, marinades and herbs is a great example of additional products to offer beyond simply meat.

■ Delete any low-quality services offered and do not cheapen your own service with poor add-on sales.

■ Create your shortlist for promotion.

4 Add dates to the shortlist so that you plan the promotion over a year. A promotion each month or one per quarter would be a great place to start.

■ For each promotion, send it to your mailing list.

■ Review your plan to avoid over-promoting to your mailing list and damaging your relationship with them.

5 Start promoting!

Key points from this chapter

■ *Effective* marketing produces leads and sales, so remember to measure the different methods tried so you can see what's worked and what hasn't and decide whether to continue with particular advertising campaigns or not.

■ Money spent on advertising that produces no leads is wasted.

- Leads turn into customers only when they decide to buy.

- Every person who walks on to your premises, calls your business or visits your website is a lead if you can capture his or her name and e-mail address.

- Successful businesses stand out from the crowd by specialising and differentiating themselves from the competition.

- Advertising needs to grab the attention of readers instantly.

- View customers as a long-term income stream, not one-off transactions.

6

Create your unstoppable sales machine

The Growth Blueprints for sales and sales management

There is only one boss. The customer. And he can fire everybody in the company from the chairman on down, simply by spending his money somewhere else.

Sam Walton, founder of Wal-Mart

At the most basic level, salespeople must bring in more revenue than they cost the business to employ them. Yet, after salespeople are recruited they are largely left to manage themselves. In the world of small business, they are rarely trained or given meaningful targets, there is no monitoring of performance and they are paid even when they don't make sales. It is easy to say that this is no way to run a business, yet, from the many businesses I have seen, 90 per cent run sales like that – even some rather successful businesses.

This chapter provides a framework for getting the best out of your sales team, including quickly fixing fundamental problems that may very well be festering away inside your team right now. For sales to work well, the right people have to be recruited, they need to manage their leads using a customer relationship management (CRM) system, follow an effective sales process and activity- and results-based targets. A salesperson kept busy doing the right things in the right way is a successful salesperson – the kind needed for your business to grow.

There are two broad aspects to achieving high-performance sales: high activity levels and robust sales methods. Putting these together, as shown in Figure 6.1, creates a professional and highly productive sales team.

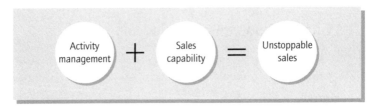

Figure 6.1   **Equation for unstoppable sales**

case notes

Darren – the owner of a financial services firm with four advisers, including himself – was frustrated that he was personally achieving half of the sales each month.

Introducing a CRM system revealed a lack of follow-up on each lead. So, activity targets were introduced to keep in touch with prospects more effectively. The team members were trained to use a rigorous sales process and sales targets were updated daily on a whiteboard. These were important factors that supported business growth of over 500 per cent in three years.

In this chapter, the sales activity management in Growth Blueprint 15 includes the systems and methods used to monitor sales activity, set targets and make visible the efforts of the sales team (including yourself if you are the only salesperson).

Create high-performance salespeople – Growth Blueprint 16 teaches you how to sell your products and services more effectively using a sales process. It also introduces key success elements for your salespeople.

Success tip

After initial induction training and a honeymoon period in the job, use a 'three strikes and you're out' rule to quickly eliminate poor salespeople. Set a minimum sales target for each month, based on them covering their own costs, including the cost of any leads they are given. If they fail to hit this target for three months in a row, they will be out.

Growth Blueprint 15: Sales activity management

Sales can be an emotionally demanding job, with the challenge of speaking to many people and retaining a positive outlook, even when no sale is made. This, when combined with the fact that they tend to operate without close supervision, can lead to them exaggerating how hard they are working and the sales they expect to make. As each month goes by and the results consistently underachieve in relation to their forecasts, the business owner loses belief and thinks that *all* salespeople behave this way.

Sales activity management will change that view. It introduces targets, measures and a system to reliably monitor these things, to ensure that sales performance can be accurately predicted and sales efforts can be managed.

Introduce a customer relationship management (CRM) system

When salespeople are dealing with a dozen or so different prospects, it is likely that they will forget what they have said to one of them or to make a follow-up call. A successful business needs a 'sales memory' to hold contact details for all leads and customers. The system will hold a history of contact with each person, including a record of phone calls and copies of e-mails that have been sent and received. It needs to have a calendar and 'to do' list to remind salespeople of actions they need to undertake to follow up sales opportunities. It should also allow you to produce reports and statistics for sales made, sales lost and other similar searches.

There is a multitude of different CRM systems available for small- to medium-sized businesses. In practice, there is a choice to be made between installing some software on your own computers and subscribing to an online service so that you can access data from anywhere. Both solutions can work, so the choice comes down to the precise requirements of your business.

Starting to use a CRM system is a culture shock for most sales-people. They will complain that it takes far too long to enter data into the system. They will complain that the system is too slow, too cumbersome or too difficult for them to use. You must, however, commit to using it and work diligently to place the CRM system at the centre of your sales operations. The benefits of having a high-quality source of data about the sales team's performance is worth the effort on its own.

case notes

A client with a call centre installed a CRM system to track sales each month for its team of 12 salespeople. A review of the number of phone calls made versus sales volumes showed a clear correlation between activity and results. The top-performing salespeople made over 60 calls per day. The lowest performer was making 28 calls each day, resulting in sales of less than 20 per cent of those of the top performers. Driving his activity up to 60 calls per day played a vital role in tripling his sales within 3 months.

Another major benefit is that if a salesperson is unwell for a period or leaves the business, his or her record of contact with customers provides a trail that can be picked up and continued, allowing sales (and, hence, business growth) to continue seamlessly and without interruption.

Hunting and farming: the two sales roles

Before getting into the details of activity management, it is useful to draw a distinction between two different roles played by salespeople. Each role is needed in different situations. By understanding these and applying them to your own business and team, you will appreciate how to use sales activity management to best effect.

Hunting is seeking out new prospects and 'making the kill'. People who excel at this are often seen as competitive and ambitious. Typical hunting activities will include attending trade shows, knocking on doors and cold calling on the phone. Those best at hunting will tend to be strong at converting marketing leads from enquiries into customers.

Farming is the activity of forming strong, long-term relationships and bonds with customers. People who excel at farming are often seen as nurturing and sociably adept. Farming activities are those that maintain client loyalty and develop them into larger accounts. Farming activities will include frequent 'social' visits to clients to get to know them better, developing personal rapport, handing out little gifts, as well as the more direct sales efforts of cross-selling and packaging up services to better suit the client and maximise revenues.

In an ideal world, hunters would go out and win new business. They would then hand these over to the farmers to manage and maintain them. In small businesses, though, it is more common for salespeople to have to be competent in both hunting *and* farming.

Manage activities and results will automatically follow

It is often said that sales is a numbers game, but what does this mean? It comes from the simple idea that the number of sales produced is a direct result of the activity that goes into it. In the earlier example, the salesperson who made just 28 calls per day was getting the worst results. By driving up his activity (the calls per day), his results improved dramatically.

Figure 6.2 shows a simplistic but powerful equation for the hunting sales activity.

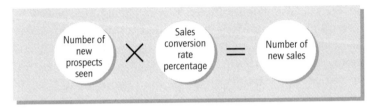

Figure 6.2 Hunting: more prospects and better sales conversion rates result in more sales

The sales conversion rate percentage is how well the salesperson sells. In Figure 6.3, there is a worked example.

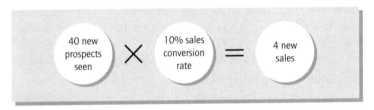

Figure 6.3 Example of how new customers are won by hunting

Figure 6.3 shows that this particular salesperson would be expected to make 4 sales if they saw 40 prospects – a 10 per cent sales conversion rate. So, if your business needs them to make 5 sales, they would need to see 50 prospects. In practice, each salesperson will perform differently and these figures can be obtained from the CRM system.

In *The Loyalty Effect: The hidden force behind growth, profits and lasting value*, Frederick F. Reichheld states that, 'A typical company's customers leave at a rate of 10% to 30% per year, and this number grows annually'. Preventing these customers from leaving makes a big difference to your annual sales.

The reason most customers leave is described in a number of studies as 'perceived indifference' – that is, they think that your business doesn't care about them. One way that some companies address this is by contacting or visiting each customer once in a while in a systematic way. This is a farming activity.

> ### Success tip
>
> Keeping in touch with customers every three months is the bare minimum required for customer retention, but figures will vary depending upon industry and the customers involved. Use CRM to monitor attrition and plan regular contact with customers, paying particular attention to important and high-value accounts.

Consider a catering business with a core of 60 regular, repeat customers each month. The priority in this business will be to protect those 60 customers from being poached by competitors. Only after *these* customers have been looked after should the salesperson begin to look for *new* customers.

In this case, it might be appropriate for the salesperson to visit all 60 customers every month, perhaps taking a taster of a new dish with her. By getting to know the customers, she can introduce additional services and products to them. These farming activities generate further opportunities and customer referrals to grow the value of sales from each account.

For farming, the activity numbers will be about reducing customer attrition, hence improving customer retention. The formula for this is shown in Figure 6.4.

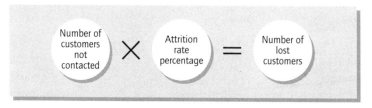

Figure 6.4 When farming is not managed, customers are lost

For example, as shown in Figure 6.5, if only ten customers receive a visit each month, five customers are lost.

Figure 6.5 Example of how customers are lost when farming is inadequate

The astute business owner will understand the business' sales process and the abilities of its salespeople and use this information to generate a strong sales plan. Key to this sales plan will be a balance of hunting versus farming activities to ensure new clients are continually acquired to satisfy growth targets, while simultaneously retaining existing customers.

The power of sales targets and a public whiteboard

Sales performance is enhanced when the members of your team can see how they are all doing, both together and individually. The simplest way to achieve this is with a whiteboard showing the value of sales, or profit produced, for each team member for the current week, month or year. Monthly targets generally work well because it resets the competition frequently enough to keep it interesting. Notice that this whiteboard is not about *activity* – that is managed by the CRM system – it displays the results that *follow* from the activity.

> ### Success tip
>
> Bonus and commission payments are powerful motivators for salespeople. Pay them frequently to closely associate the reward with the achievement of goals. A bonus that is added up during the year and paid at the end will have far less motivational impact for most people than one paid monthly.

Figure 6.6 gives an example of a whiteboard that one client uses very successfully. The dark horizontal line represents a breakeven sales level of £8500. Salespeople know that they have to rise above this line consistently to keep their jobs.

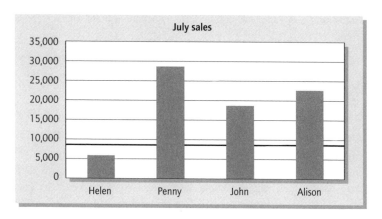

Figure 6.6 Example of whiteboard targets for a sales team

Salespeople will commonly have a competitive streak in their nature. The chance to look good in front of their colleagues will drive the top performers even harder, while the rest of the pack will work hard to avoid being at the bottom. You can make it really hit home by showing the minimum acceptable sales performance, too. The board will become a natural gathering point for the members of your sales team, who will jockey for position on it and compete with each other to avoid being bottom or to have the top sales figures for the month.

Success tip

Performance can be increased further with friendly competitions. Offer prizes for different categories – like best conversion rate, biggest individual sale, best sales team (split them into groups for this), Top Gun salesperson and so on. This will shift the intensity up another notch and sales will improve as a direct result.

Breakthrough Action Plan 15: Sales activity management

Get control over your sales performance by actioning these simple steps.

1 Invest in a CRM system to manage your leads and customers. Download the free report about CRM systems at www.double-your-business.com for guidance on how to choose a CRM system that will provide the right support for both sales and marketing.

2 Set targets for the value of sales required.

3 Calculate how much activity will be needed to deliver those sales targets, split clearly between hunting and farming activities. Look at your customer base to decide how much focus needs to be given to hunting versus farming.

   ■ Set activity targets for hunting activities based on the number of sales appointments that must be attended each week or month to achieve the sales target.

   ■ Set activity targets for farming activities based on contacting every customer in some way at least once per quarter.

   ■ Have the CRM system set up to produce reports to show both activity levels and results, in terms of sales revenues, for both of the above.

4 Hold monthly sales reviews.

   ■ Have all salespeople completed the right number of activities?

   ■ Have all salespeople achieved their targets?

5 Calculate the minimum sales required from each salesperson in order for them to comfortably cover their own costs.

   ■ Include pay and any employment tax, vehicle and fuel expenses, phones, office space and an appropriate proportion of marketing costs for any leads they are given.

   ■ Add 20 per cent to cover your time as a management overhead.

   ■ Set a minimum sales target for your 'three strikes and out' rule.

   ■ Hold a sales meeting to introduce the targets and new rules.

6 Put up a whiteboard in a public area and write the minimum sales targets on it.

- ■ Update the figures on a regular basis – whenever a sale is made or daily if many sales are being made.

- ■ Frequently talk about performance and generate some buzz about top sales performers.

- ■ Introduce prizes and rewards for good performance.

Growth Blueprint 16: Create high-performance salespeople

The idea of there being natural born salespeople is a fallacy, arising from the mistaken belief that a good salesperson is somebody who can talk persuasively. While persuasion is one part of selling, a lot has to happen before a customer will be ready to be persuaded.

In this Growth Blueprint the two key aspects of high-performance sales are brought together. First, we look at why normal recruitment methods often fail to find good salespeople and offer some alternative ideas for reversing this situation. Then, the four-step sales process is explained – how selling can be broken down into the logical, simple steps of connecting, understanding, presenting and selling.

How to recruit high-performance salespeople

A frequent frustration for the owners or managers of businesses is that they cannot find good salespeople. In truth, very good salespeople can choose where they want to work, will earn good bonuses and only change jobs for a considerably better reward. If you want to recruit a high-performing salesperson with extensive experience in your particular field, you will likely be looking for a needle in a haystack. There are three sensible choices open, although the first one rarely produces results.

Follow the normal recruitment process

This means that you will spend a lot of time talking to poor performers and trying to find what quality there is in the pile of applications that come in for sales jobs. Many of the people who apply will be average or below-average performers because few Top Guns will be out looking for jobs.

Grow your own talent

This is a great option if you understand sales and are willing to invest the time and energy to train a new salesperson from scratch. All you have to do is find somebody with the fundamental qualities, which are explained later on.

Approach top salespeople directly

This is an aggressive strategy that produces the best results. A professional headhunter will be able to do this discretely for you.

Traits of high-performing salespeople

From many years observing and working with great salespeople, plus insights from an advanced psychological profiling tool, I have arrived at several key traits that every consistently high-performing salesperson will demonstrate. These are in no particular order, but of equal importance.

High levels of self-confidence people buy from people, and confident people (not arrogant) are great people to be with.

Willingness to argue their point when prospects raise some problems or issues with a sale, salespeople must not shrivel, but stand tall and fight their corner without becoming aggressive.

Persistence and resilience there will be a great many leads who don't buy. The best salespeople have a thick skin that can take the inevitable knocks.

Ambitious all good performers will have some ambition – great salespeople will be more ambitious than most, having a real hunger, a 'fire in their belly' driving them.

Competitive top salespeople like to win; it's what drives them. That is why sales competitions are such a great tool for driving higher levels of performance from sales teams.

High standards solid performers set high standards for themselves and those around them. This keeps them sharp and ensures they pay attention to the details that make extra sales happen.

Maturity high performers keep their cool when customers behave unpredictably. They project a consistently professional image and will keep sales rolling in.

First impression high performers will make a strong impression on first meeting – clearly an essential trait for selling.

How to sell – the four-step sales process

People cannot be forced to buy something. If you have products and services that are of real value to your customers, this sales process will help you to effortlessly sell more than ever before. I have taught this process to retailers, accountants, printers, carpet cleaners, salespeople for office furniture, mortgage brokers, heating engineers and countless other professions besides. It is simple to understand, easy to learn and incredibly effective.

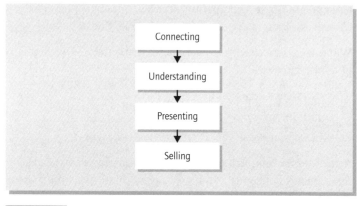

Figure 6.7 The four-step sales process

The sales process has four steps (see Figure 6.7). Each of these includes details that are important to selling successfully. Following the outline of the four stages as a guide will help your sales force to improve, while mastering the details within each step will take them to another level altogether.

Success tip

To help your people learn and master this sales process, ask them to try recording a few sales meetings and study them afterwards. By listening carefully to these recordings, they will notice details that either hinder or help their sales. This is one of the fastest ways to improve their sales performance.

Connecting

Millions of years of evolution have honed our survival instincts to make judgement calls about the people we trust and those we don't. Before people will buy a product or service, they must first feel comfortable enough to trust the salesperson.

My father was a salesperson in the 1960s for a specialist engineering company. One of his customers was a major car manufacturer. He explained that, when you arrived at their factory, you were directed to one of two car parks – one nearby if you drove the cars they made themselves; another, much further away, if you drove a competitor's car. The message was very clear: we will welcome you only if you are on our side.

When we connect with somebody, we trust them. The elements of connecting are:

- a strong first impression
- common ground
- minimise anxiety.

A strong first impression happens in the moment a salesperson first meets somebody. Studies suggest that first impressions will not change for the next 20 interactions, so the impact made in that first meeting will set the scene for success or failure. Salespeople must start by dressing appropriately for the customers. So, if your product is surfboards, don't let your salespeople wear a suit and tie, but if you have £10,000 bespoke computer systems, the salespeople shouldn't wear t-shirts and shorts. For retail businesses, uniforms are a great way to support your brand image and help customers to easily spot your sales staff. Shaking hands firmly is a skill to be taught. Your salespeople can't use either a gorilla grip or the dreaded floppy fish! Personal grooming and fresh breath complete the mix.

The common ground element is about establishing a bond between the customer and the salesperson. Humans are tribal by nature, so we tend to trust those who have something in common with us far more than people we know nothing about. Your sales-people must begin, during their initial conversations, to find something that they have in common with each customer. Have them look for clues – the customer's car keys, pictures on the desk or walls and so on. The idea is not to *falsely* show interest in them (a tactic that's obvious when done without integrity), but genuinely seek a connection to develop some common ground.

It is important to minimise anxiety because, even when we are buying something for ourselves, we don't like the experience of being sold to. Robert's mobile phone rang and the caller launched right into the dialogue: 'Hello Robert, how has your day been?' Robert snapped back, 'Whatever you are selling, I am not interested. My day has been *very* busy and I don't appreciate salespeople ringing me and calling me by my first name!' The caller responded, 'Oh, I am just returning the call you made this morning, requesting an appointment to have new tyres fitted to your car.' We all share the same scepticism about salespeople.

So, it's best to eliminate this anxiety at the start of sales meetings by telling customers exactly what to expect. Start by explaining the four-step sales process to the client in simple terms, something like this. 'First, I'd like to take just 30 seconds to tell you a little bit about our business and what we do. Then I'll ask some questions so I can understand what you are looking for. We can then look at ways that my business can help. Finally, if we agree there is a match between what you need and our products, we can discuss moving forwards. How does that sound?'

This may seem a bold gambit, but it defuses a great deal of tension because the customer now understands precisely how the meeting will work. It also takes the pressure off for the moment because the customer knows that the salesperson will not be selling until the very end. The customer can raise his or her guard again then, but, for now, will feel far safer and the salesperson will be able to have an open and effective conversation as a result.

Understanding

Once a connection has been made, before any selling can be done, your salespeople need to understand what each customer actually needs, as well as his or her emotional trigger for wanting to buy. Research into decision making has shown that our brain's emotional centre, the amygdala, plays a major part when we have to make up our minds about anything. Even for the smallest of decisions, like whether or not you should try a new type of cereal, the emotional centre of your brain is consulted.

This part of the sales process has three parts:

- open questions
- active listening
- confirm hot buttons.

case notes

A customer came into a jewellery shop asking for a plain, square-faced watch suitable for a child. She had looked all over town for one and drawn a blank. The well-trained sales assistant asked her questions about why she wanted such a specific type of watch and listened carefully to the woman's answers. By the time she left the shop ten minutes later, she was a very happy customer. She bought a round-faced Manchester United watch for her football-mad grandson's tenth birthday, to help him learn to tell the time. It had never occurred to the woman to buy him a watch linked to his favourite football team and she was truly delighted to have a novel solution to her problem.

A few basic questions can produce a sale and a very happy customer. The example in the case notes box, while incredibly simple, shows how a good salesperson solves problems for customers. By asking open-ended questions and listening carefully to the answers, a great salesperson discovers exactly what the customer needs and helps them to buy it.

Open questions are those that start with 'Who?', 'What?', 'Where?', 'When?' or 'How?' They are 'open' because the answers to these questions cannot be a simple 'Yes' or 'No'. They open up the conversation and encourage the customer to talk. The more time and effort customers put into explaining their problems, needs and wants, the more chance your salesperson will have of understanding them. Here are some examples of open questions that might be used to help somebody to buy a car.

- '*What* types of car interest you the most?'
- '*Where* will you be driving your new car?'
- '*Who* will be travelling with you in your car?'

When selling, the goal is to find out precisely what people want, so the questions will start out being general and gradually become more specific as the salesperson narrows down to find the precise needs. It is perfectly sensible to ask more detailed questions, for example, to discover if the customer has a preference for diesel or petrol engines.

A wise salesperson I knew stuck to the motto 'You have two ears and one mouth – use them in that proportion'. He was one of the most successful salespeople that I have come across. It is not enough to just stop talking while your customer answers your questions. You have to *actively* listen to what they are saying if you want to fully understand the needs they are looking to fulfil. Your salespeople need to become 'listening machines'. The more intently they listen, the more they will pick up on the precise words that customers use, as well as visual cues from their body language.

Active listening includes giving feedback to the speaker that shows they have been heard. This is done through verbal and visual cues, such as nodding of the head and reassuring sounds and words. The most effective feedback will be actions that encourage further talking – things like, 'Mmm', 'Ah, I see' and 'Please go on'. Another technique is to repeat back to them what they have said in order to confirm understanding.

The understanding stage becomes a cycle of questions and listening, with answers raising more questions to help the salesperson reach the heart of customers' needs and motivations. Motivation is important because it is the emotional trigger needed for the sale. It takes a series of open questions and active listening to appreciate what customers want (the need) and why this matters to them (the motivation).

Once the question and listening cycle has been completed salespeople need to demonstrate their understanding of their customers' needs by summarising them in a simple statement, highlighting the important, emotionally charged elements shared by customers during the active listening phase.

To demonstrate how the understanding step typically works, here is an example based on an imagined conversation between a customer and a salesperson in a camera shop.

Customer: 'I am looking for a new digital camera.'

Salesperson: 'Certainly, sir – my name is Adam. What did you have in mind?'

Customer: 'I have been reading the magazines, and the new Canon SLR appeals, but I have only previously had a point and shoot camera, so I don't know if I'll be able to handle it. I am not very technically minded, you see.'

Salesperson: 'OK, well, before we get into the details of camera choice, would it be OK if I asked a few questions to help us find a few options that could suit you?'

Customer: 'Yes, that would be helpful.'

Salesperson: 'OK, so the first thing we need to do is understand what you expect to be using the camera for.'

Customer: 'Well, I like walking and I have taken a few landscape pictures recently that are beautiful, but a friend told me that the lens on these little cameras can distort around the edges. He's a real camera buff and told me I need an SLR.'

Salesperson: 'Ah, so you like landscape photography. It sounds like you are pretty keen, if you are considering a new camera to take even better photos. Is there any particular reason why you want to get rid of this distortion?'

Customer: 'I frame some of the pictures I take and put them on the walls around the house, because they are great reminders of the wonderful times I have when walking. Since my friend told me about the distortion, it is spoiling the memory for me.'

Salesperson: 'From what you have told me, you are looking for a camera with the following features. First, it must be <u>easy to carry when you are walking</u>. Second, it must have an <u>excellent lens for landscape photography so that it eliminates distortion</u> that could spoil the memories of your walks. Finally, you need something with <u>simple settings</u> as you don't want something that's overly complicated and technical. Is there anything else that is important to you?'

Customer: 'No, I think that is everything, thanks.'

From this example conversation, you can see how the salesperson asks a few questions to understand what the customer wants, but, more than this, the salesperson has also discovered the emotion – the current camera is distorting the pictures and spoiling the customer's memories. Hence, the customer has a specific motivation to buy a new camera. Without training, most salespeople would pick up on the product name – 'the new Canon SLR' – mentioned at the start of the dialogue and then try hard to persuade the customer to buy it.

At this point, though, our salesperson is ready to move on to the next stage of the sales process.

Presenting

Once salespeople understand what customers need, their task is to match up the appropriate products and services to satisfy them. It is important not to rush to get to the presentation because, if the needs and motivation are not properly understood, making a sale becomes less likely. In fact, one of the biggest factors that *prevents* sales is leaping into the presentation before customers' needs are understood. The presenting step has three key elements:

- options
- presentation
- choice.

Options are when customers are provided with more than one viable option. This will give them a sense of being the decision-maker and not being railroaded into a forced solution. Letting them review several alternatives, in fact, will generally increase sales. By highlighting the specific features that press their hot buttons, customers will be reassured that the salesperson has listened and will be confident that the suggested solutions will be a good match for them.

Here's how this might work for the camera example.

Salesperson: 'There are two main options for you. One would be the Canon SLR camera your friend recommended. It has settings for different kinds of pictures, including a landscape mode that is designed to set the camera properly for the kinds of pictures you take. This will be perfect for you because it makes the Canon almost as easy to use as your point and shoot camera. The option to put different lenses on it means that you can even use the same lens as professional landscape photographers, giving you spectacular pictures without any distortion. Your memories will be perfectly preserved with this option. With a waterproof, lightweight camera bag, it will be easy for you to take on your walks.'

Customer: 'That sounds great. What is the other option?'

Salesperson: 'The second option is to go for an upmarket all-in-one camera. These cameras are smaller and lighter and come with a carry case, so they will be easy to carry when walking. They are built around a high-quality lens, which will be a big improvement on what you have now, although not quite as good as the other option. They are very simple to use, too. They are a great middle-ground option and £150 cheaper than the Canon SLR.'

By providing a choice of two options that both satisfy customers' needs, while explaining the differences between them, customers feel in control of the ultimate decision as to what is best for them.

Presentation is straightforward when selling something tangible, like the camera in the example. It is easy to demonstrate it directly to customers and let them explore it for themselves. The item itself is the star of the presentation.

What about selling something that is intangible, like accountancy services? For these, some kind of presentation material will help to engage customers. Materials must be professional and cover all the services you sell. For example, an accountant might have a set of slides that describes the business, with a slide for each major service area, like bookkeeping, payroll, tax advice and so on. Remember also to include some testimonials for your service, since they provide proof that other people like what you do.

Choice is offering customers a low number of solutions as the first step to gaining their commitment, which leads to the final stage of the sales process. It provides an opportunity to test whether or not these solutions have addressed customers' needs and, if not, the chance to have another go. Simply say something like, 'So which of these do you think will be the best fit for you?' then wait in silence for their answer.

Success tip

Although it might seem more helpful to offer up many choices to customers, the result will be confusion. Studies have shown that the more options people are given, the less able they become to choose.

My strong recommendation is to offer just two choices. It is much easier for customers to compare two items and choose one over the other than to mentally juggle half a dozen options.

Selling

A sale is only complete when customers pay or make a firm commitment in the form of a signature on a contract. It does not matter how enthusiastic customers have been, if they don't finally sign on the dotted line, no sale has been made.

The selling step of the sales process helps your salespeople to close the deal. It comprises three parts:

- ask softly for the sale
- handle objections
- take payment.

When customers indicate a preference for one option over another, it hopefully means they are ready to buy, but it may just be that they are moving one step *closer* to buying. Asking softly for the sale is how the salesperson finds out whether or not the customer is ready to buy. Here are five ways to ask softly for a sale.

- Would you like to pay by cash or credit card?
- We just need to sort out the paperwork now – could I take your address, please?
- Where would you like it to be delivered?
- When would be a good time for us to meet and get started?
- Would you like it gift-wrapped?

When customers do not want to go ahead, it means that they have some kind of objection, which can be managed in the following manner.

Objections are questions, not the precursor to a lost sale. Typical objections include price, having to speak to a spouse or partner before committing, plus technical questions and so on. It's also common for people to want to go away and think a little before making their purchase decision.

Some customers will use one objection as a smokescreen to cover for something that they are too embarrassed to admit. For example, if they say, 'I need to think about it', they may really be thinking it's too expensive or that they want to shop around first. When they give an objection, have your salespeople check that that is really the issue by repeating it back to them and asking if it is the only thing stopping them from buying right now. A conversation might go like this.

Customer: 'I need to speak to my wife before buying it.'

Salesperson: 'So, if I understand correctly, what you are saying is that your wife has a say in the decision to buy?'

Customer: 'Yes, she controls the purse strings in our house and this is a little more expensive than I agreed with her.'

Salesperson: 'Ah, OK, so to check my understanding, what you are saying is that this solution is over your budget?'

Customer: 'Yes, it is really, I had agreed with my wife to spend no more than £500.'

Salesperson: 'So if we could find a way to get the price under £500, we could do the deal right away?'

You can see here that the salesperson is getting to the bottom of the objection and may indeed be able to do some kind of negotiation to bring the price to a point that a sale can be made. The secret with objections is to treat them as the *start* of a *discussion*, not the *end* of the *sale*.

Once the objection has been handled, it is time to repeat the closing questions and secure payment or the customer's signature on the sales agreement.

Breakthrough Action Plan 16: Create high-performance salespeople

Follow these steps to improve sales skills in your sales team.

1 Recruit your next salesperson differently:

- headhunt a top performer

- identify an existing employee to advance into sales through training and mentoring.

2 Have your salespeople record sales conversations using a portable voice recorder or dictation device. They will need to explain to customers that they are making some training materials and want to record themselves. Have each salesperson replay their tapes, privately, and take action to improve their interaction skills.

3 Check your salespeople against the four-step sales process and take action to improve their skills in:

- connecting

- understanding

- presenting

- selling.

Key points from this chapter

- An unstoppable sales machine is essential for the growth of your business.

- A CRM system is the 'sales memory' for your business.

- Salespeople need to be busy doing the right activities all the time.

- Recruit salespeople who have a track record of sales success.

- Underperforming salespeople will hinder your business growth.

- The robust four-step sales process forms must be the backbone of sales improvement.

Systems to make your business work without you

The Growth Blueprints to stabilise, systemise and optimise your business

If you can't describe what you are doing as a process, you don't know what you're doing.

W. Edwards Deming

I f you were to watch master cabinetmakers designing, preparing and building a piece of furniture from the roughly cut wood, you would marvel at their creative skills and consider them artists. Yet, if you were to watch them do so over and over again, you would notice a clear sequence of steps that were taken to bring their art into the world. From the time taken looking at the wood to inspire their creative muscles, to the caressing of the plane's blade to bring it to a razor's edge on a sharpening stone, every single action is part of a definite production sequence followed every time.

A *system*, then, is a predetermined sequence that will predictably achieve a result. In a business, once you have documented your systems into procedures, you can train your employees and, with practice, they will perform their work without constantly referring back to you. If you let your team come to you with every issue, you are training dependence on you into them. There needs to be a system to instruct employees in every aspect of how the business runs. This system is your operations manual and is created in Growth Blueprint 18, presented in this chapter.

Of course, if there are constant interruptions due to problems and you cannot get an hour at a time to work on things, there will be little chance for you to ever systemise your business. The elimination of such constant firefighting is tackled when you stabilise your business, as described in Growth Blueprint 17 in this chapter.

Finally, when your business has become fully systemised and is running smoothly, there will be time for you to look for ways to grow with less effort when you optimise your business, as described in Growth Blueprint 19. Figure 7.1 shows how these three Growth Blueprints fit together.

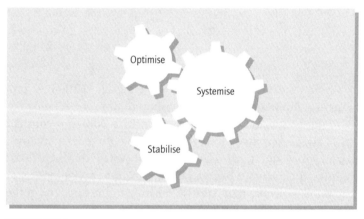

Figure 7.1   The three stages of systemising your business

Success tip

Successfully introducing systems to your business is not something you will achieve overnight. Your staff will need time to learn and use them. They will also avoid using them sometimes, if there are short cuts. You will need to be a strong leader to offer encouragement when they are struggling and discipline when they can't be bothered. You will also need to be a role model and always use the systems yourself – if *you* take short cuts, you are telling your members of staff that it's OK for them to take short cuts, too.

Growth Blueprint 17: Stabilise to eliminate firefighting

When you cannot sit and work for 45 minutes without being interrupted to answer questions, deal with customer issues or answer the phone, you are in firefighting mode. You'll recognise the symptoms of being unable to concentrate on anything for long, being driven by the reactive nature of your business and having a feeling of burnout from not knowing how much longer you can keep it up. While this is going on, it's impossible to make a big push on sales (or anything else) because you are so limited by how little you can get done each day.

Your priority when the business is doing this to you is to stabilise your business with very simple systems like checklists, to help you quickly gain control.

Identify the biggest, most expensive and most distracting problems

If you have serious firefighting problems, you will find it easy to make a list of the different types of problems that happen. If you can remember all of the problems from the past week, write them down on a blank sheet of paper with the title 'Firefighting issues' at the top of the page. The idea here is to get an accurate view of the different types of problems that are hurting your business. If you can't remember, simply track them during the coming week as they happen.

If firefighting is a symptom, the only way to get out of the vicious cycle is to figure out why the problems happen in the first place. Sometimes a single problem can produce many different visible symptoms. While you might be able to fix or prevent some of them in isolation, it would be like putting a bucket under water dripping from the ceiling – it doesn't actually fix anything, it just stores up trouble for another day. Once you have got a list, pick one of the issues that is the most annoying to you – something that happens a lot and causes all kinds of disruption would be a great place to start.

Ask 'Why?' to find out the root cause of your problems

Having identified a problem, the key to eliminating it is getting to the heart of it. In the case of the drip from a ceiling, it might be a leaking pipe, an overflow from a sink, a broken roof tile or a spilt drink on the floor above.

To do this, you can use root cause analysis, which means you keep asking 'Why?' until you find the root of the problem and a solution for it. Here is how this technique might be used to discover why an item regularly runs out of stock in a business.

- *Issue: No black ink available at the start of a working day at a stationery printing company*
    - Why? We had used the supply up over the past few days.
    - Why? Because we use it daily on practically every job and nobody thought to restock it.
    - Why? Because the boss normally does this when he's here.
    - Why? Because he has always placed all the orders ever since he started the business.
    - Why? Because he doesn't think anybody else can do it properly.
    - Why? Because only he knows how much we will normally use.
    - Why? Because there is no minimum stock level to trigger an order for ink so that we never run out.

Notice that 'Why?' is asked seven times before we get to an actionable answer, where a system problem can be given a permanent fix. Until then, it would have been easy to think it was the staff being deliberately awkward and letting it happen. In truth, there just needs to be a little bit of thought given to solving any problem like this.

> ### Success tip
>
> When something goes wrong it's natural for people to become defensive. Asking 'Who?' is likely to cause defensiveness in people, making the problem even harder to overcome. The best way to get past this is to ask for your team's help to solve problems and identify root causes. Saying, 'Hey guys, this problem has happened three times this month – anybody got any ideas what's causing this, so we can figure out a way to fix it together?' is much more likely to produce a positive result.

The power of checklists and other simple systems

One argument I sometimes hear when trying to encourage people to introduce systems is that their employees are highly skilled, professionally qualified people and simple systems would be beneath them. If this happens to you (or if you feel this way yourself), then this next story will help.

A few years ago, the media reported that surgeons at eight different hospitals had used a checklist to improve operation success rates. They reduced deaths from complications arising from surgery by 40 per cent. These are some of the most highly qualified individuals on the planet, yet the checklists were ridiculously simple – things like counting the number of dressings and tools used and confirming that they were all accounted for before stitching the patient back together. It turns out that it is very common, with all the mess of operating, for bits of surgical paraphernalia to be left inside patients.

How much could checklists help you, too? In practice, I find that the right checklist can eliminate many of the problems that clients have faced on a regular basis, because they effectively transfer ownership of a system problem to the employees, eliminating the wriggle space of human error they would normally use to say, 'I forgot that'. They either follow the checklist or they don't. If they don't, there is either a training issue or a disciplinary matter to pursue.

case notes

Colin runs a commercial vehicle repair business with a reputation for quality.

Over a coffee, he asked for my help. 'Why are my staff so utterly helpless when I am not in the office?' he asked, 'I couldn't turn my phone off for five minutes while I was on holiday. They were constantly interrupting me for help with every little thing. After just two weeks away, the business was at a virtual standstill. Without me, my team have no appreciation that customers need to be looked after and no clue what they are doing in their daily work!'

We spent some time exploring why this happened and a pattern quickly emerged. Here are some of the issues that the team had called him about.

- How could they get spare parts delivered for a rush job that *they* had agreed to do?
- What should they do with a customer who has refused to pay on the basis that he disputed the need for some of the repairs?
- Which customers could they cancel appointments with, because they had booked too many jobs in?
- Was it OK to do a courier order for engine oil, since it ran out of stock?

His team simply had no idea how to run the business in his absence. A simple system to handle job planning solved many issues, a simple stock control system ensured oil and other consumables were always available and some written guidelines to deal with difficult customers completed the changes. His team members were then trained to use the new methods and, when problems occurred, rather than going to Colin for answers, they were able to solve the majority on their own.

There are many simple things you can do to quickly eliminate the root cause of your problems. Here are three other ways that I've shown clients – they helped them to quickly solve many of their daily problems. An example is given in each case.

- Signs that instruct people what to do at just the right moment (e.g. a line marked on the side of a bottle to indicate the reorder level).

- Forms with spaces for all the information that needs to be captured. The example in Figure 7.2 shows a lead capture form used to collect the details of people who call in with a sales enquiry of any kind. Notice how the 'First name' line reminds them to confirm the spelling of the caller's name. This type of form quickly prevents problems of missing or incorrect data.

Enquiry lead capture form	
Date	
First name (spelling!)	
Surname	
Company name	
E-mail address	
Mobile number	
Office number	
Nature of enquiry	Service I New purchase I Info pack
Where did they hear about us?	Web I Customer I Newspaper
Comments	

Figure 7.2 Example of an enquiry lead capture form created to capture all information consistently

- Whiteboards in your office can be used to show charts, priorities, checklists, rotas, responsibilities and a host of other things, improving communication among your team members and making your business run more smoothly. The example in Figure 7.3 shows a whiteboard set up for a letting agency to track progress for new properties coming in for letting. The properties are listed down the left and the stage reached in the process across the top. A daily review immediately shows any hold-ups and the public nature of the whiteboard introduces accountability.

Property	Landlord instructed	Inspected and accepted	Photographed	Ad created	Advertised	Tenant vetted	Contract and inventory	Deposit and direct debit taken	Property let
47 Castle Street	✓	✓	✓	✓	✓	✓	✓	✓	✓
88 Bellencroft Gdns	✓	✓	✓	✓	✓	✓			
501 Willenhall Rd	✓	✓	✓	✓	✓	✓	✓	✓	
194 Windsor Av.	✓	✓	✓						

Figure 7.3 Example of a whiteboard used to track progress through a number of steps

Just find simple, practical ways to communicate the key facts to your team at the right time for them to take action. When you do this, your team members will develop new, useful habits and appear to have a great deal more common sense, too. You will be surprised just how easily you can solve many of your regular issues.

Success tip

When your team interrupts you to ask a question for which the answer is already posted in the workplace, walk out of your office, take the employee to the operations manual and get them to read the answer to you. It won't take long for them to get the message!

Daily operations meeting

A ten-minute meeting each morning can be used to gather round a whiteboard and discuss potential issues before they blow up.

The idea is to use these short, sharp meetings to keep attention on the simple systems you develop to prevent firefighting. The meetings are a key ingredient in making things run smoothly for you.

Breakthrough Action Plan 17: Stabilise to eliminate firefighting

Here are the steps you need to take to stop problems in their tracks.

1 Make a list of the problems that most commonly interrupt you.

2 Sort these to identify the most frequent, costly or disruptive issues.

3 Use the concept of root cause analysis to diagnose the real issue behind all of the visible symptoms – that is, keep asking 'Why?' until you find something that can be actioned.

4 Create the simplest possible solutions to solve them. Use checklists, signs, forms or any other easy-to-introduce methods. Ask your team for help with finding a solution if you can't figure out how to do it yourself.

5 Schedule regular operational meetings to review how the changes are working and to make any changes to keep the fires from igniting.

Growth Blueprint 18: Systemise to create your operations manual

I had the opportunity to visit the Aston Martin car manufacturing plant with one of my clients to see how the cars are made. The manufacturing process involves a series of stages, with parts added and checks for quality happening at each point. Each car is made in the same sequence so that the employees know precisely what they need to do at each stage of the process. It's a wonderfully calm experience to watch the row of cars gradually being assembled and rolled (or driven) from stage to stage until, finally, the engines roar as they are taken off to be delivered to their new owners.

The end result is that customers know they will get a car to cherish from Aston Martin, made to exacting standards and including all the details that they have specified, right down to the colour of the stitching on the leather seats. This could not happen without systems and procedures. Your business can be just the same when you take the time to create effective systems to make sure your customers get the quality of service and products that you want them to receive, time after time.

Identify your major business processes

Every business has some major functions that define the customer experience. The consistency with which these processes run defines the quality of your products and the standard of service that your customers expect from you.

Here are some examples of the details of major processes that a business-to-consumer (B2C) outlet, like a shop or a restaurant, might need to write down to ensure consistency.

- **Opening checklist** to make sure that everything is clean and set up as you want before any customers arrive.
- **Customer care list** how your staff should look after your customers.
- **Closing checklist** what needs to be put away, how to set the alarm and lock up, etc.
- **Stock check** know how much stock you have and whether or not you need to reorder.
- **Cash reconciliation** balancing the cash in the till against the list of items sold during the day.
- **Deposit takings at bank** how cash is to be handled securely and by whom.
- **Goods received** check that your suppliers are delivering everything on their invoices.
- **Complaints procedure** what to do in the event of a customer not being satisfied.
- **Staff recruitment and induction** retailers frequently need to replace staff, so systemise how this is done to make it part of routine operations.

To systemise your business, you are going to need a list of your main processes. Shut your office door, take a sheet of paper and spend as long as it takes to make a list of the major processes. It will probably take around 45 minutes to come up with your first real hit list. You will add a few more as time goes by and you spot other areas of your business that would benefit from defined processes, too.

Once you have your master list of processes, pick one and you are ready for the next stage. It's important that you focus on a single process and complete it before moving on to the next one.

Gather the facts

Before you can create a process, you need to establish what will be involved. Gather together every fact, thought or idea you can that relates to this process. Ask your team members to contribute their ideas if you are stuck for thoughts. It is vital that you pull together your facts because the way your business runs is going to change based on the information you gather.

To return to the process ideas we looked at in the previous section, imagine you are building a process for the daily opening routine for your restaurant. You would gather all your thoughts about what needs to be done: a float for the till, stock check for food, menu update for any dishes of the day, wine cellar and wet goods (drinks) check, clean windows, mop floors, lay tables, put out clean tablecloths, clean serviettes, take the phone off the answering service, place tags on any reserved tables, etc.

Draft the process

Now, with all your gathered information, you need to put it together into some kind of sensible sequence. These steps will be your new process.

There are a few ways to document your process, the easiest of which is often the checklist, covered in the first step – the stabilise phase. For your full processes, however, there are some other ways, too. These are:

- written procedures, using a word processor or presentation software
- flowcharts
- diagrams
- screen captures (pictures of your computer screen showing each step in detail)
- video captures (video of your computer screen showing you doing the process, step by step).

There are no rules about how you should write your procedures. Feel free to have numbered instruction sheets stuck to the walls in your business and train your staff to go through them in sequence. Indeed, this can sometimes be the best way to make sure the procedure is followed. Procedures stored in a clean folder or filing cabinet will never be used!

Review the process with your team

Once you have written your process, it needs to be checked out by the most experienced or trusted people, including those who will be using it to run your business for you. Gather your team members and ask them to look through the process critically. Their job is to critique it for you – to find the cracks and problems and help you deal with them. The idea is that they will help you make the process bulletproof.

Don't take their feedback personally – think of it as their chance to engage in the process and take ownership from you, make it their own. In fact, the more improvements and changes they suggest, the better, because it is them taking a real interest in the business' operating systems. This will translate to a high degree of ownership when the process is put into practice – the people who gave feedback will not want to see their ideas fail. As a result of this, you must try to not be defensive and let them make whatever changes they feel will make it better.

As long as their changes do not damage the outcome of what the process is meant to achieve, you will get far more loyalty if you give them a free rein than if you try to micro-manage everything about it. This might mean they want to type it up in a different format, print it using pink ink or turn it into a series of posters and have them on the walls. Don't sweat the small stuff, though – let them help you make your business a more productive place.

> ### Success tip
>
> The commonest reason for processes failing is that they don't get used – people continue as they have always done and don't make the effort to change their working habits. You can overcome this by making staff record that they have followed the procedure at critical points. Taking measurements, recording the time, signing their initials are all ways to confirm that the procedure is being followed.

Develop any resources required for your process

Sometimes the introduction of a new process requires special forms to be created or in and out trays for paperwork to be stored as things move from one stage to another. You cannot put the process into play before these resources are available or else the process won't work properly, so spend the time required to prepare any extra resources before it is put into practice. A poorly implemented process will be just as likely to fail as no process at all.

Consider things such as forms, trays, signage and anything else to make your new process the way things work in your business.

Test your process

Everything should now be ready for your new process to be tested. Try it out with your team and see how it works. Fine-tune the details and again give your team members the space and freedom to tweak things if necessary – if it makes their working with the process easier, it's good for you, too.

Finally, a word about introducing processes in a bigger business. As mentioned earlier, the main reason processes don't work for you is that the staff are not trained properly to use them. Take your team members through the process and give them time to learn it properly. Let them make mistakes as they learn and gently correct them. Do not shout and bawl as they are learning – remember that a baby must fall over many times before learning to walk. If your team members make mistakes while they are learning, it's a sign that they need more practice and support to get used to the new ways of working. Once they are up to speed, your business will run more smoothly than ever before.

If your team members are OK with the way a process works, congratulations on developing a professional process.

Go live!

Now the process is ready to be put into real use. At this point, the team members will need to monitor carefully to identify gaps that weren't spotted when the process was being developed and tested. Review it after a few runs through the process and gather comments. Keep a page for notes to capture any ideas or problems and discuss them with the main users of the process, agree improvements and keep monitoring.

After a few weeks or months, the process will simply become the way that job gets done in your business. As you repeat the cycle with the next process, your business will become completely systemised within a matter of months and it will work the same whether you are there are not.

Breakthrough Action Plan 18: Systemise to create your operations manual

These are the steps you need to take to stop problems in their tracks.

1 Make a list of your major business processes.

2 Gather your facts, knowledge and ideas to feed into your new process.

3 Draft a process that pulls together the research and brainstorming you did in the previous step.

4 Review the process with your team. Give them as much freedom as possible to contribute to its development.

5 Decide how you will build accountability into the process by introducing measurements or signatures.

6 Put in place any extra resources you will need for the newly created process to work.

7 Perform a test run to see how it works, again giving your team freedom to refine and tweak it.

8 Support your team as they start using it, making sure everybody is trained adequately and is allowed to make mistakes as they get used to the new way of working.

9 Rinse and repeat – go through each of your major processes until you have systemised your whole business.

Growth Blueprint 19: Optimise your business for efficiency

When you have created all the processes for your business and have them up and running, there is another step that can transform productivity and profitability. Every business has lots of things that eat more time, energy and profit than they should. By taking time to identify these and then optimise them out of your business, it is possible to see massive leaps in profit. The challenge, though, is that this is an incredibly broad topic and will require some real focus to spot opportunities.

When I took my car to the local tyre replacement centre, they took an hour to replace 2 tyres, yet a top Formula 1 pit crew can put four new tyres on a grand prix car in 4 seconds – that's *900 times faster!* The reason that F1 teams work so hard to keep their pit stops so short is that races are won and lost on fractions of a second. A fast pit stop frequently allows one driver to jump ahead of another, so all F1 teams try to find ways to get an edge and be faster in the pits.

Business is just the same. A company that can do a job in half the time or for half the cost can operate with higher profit margins and therefore afford to invest more money in out-competing its competition. A business like that is going to be hard to beat, but it can be created when you choose to optimise your operations.

In practice, every business has some elements that take a lot of time or produce a lot of waste or somehow consume valuable resources in a way that can be eliminated. This Growth Blueprint explains how you can find these areas in your business and eliminate them.

Identify targets to optimise

It is not possible to optimise every part of a business in one go – a decision must be made about where to focus in order to get the biggest return for your efforts. The challenge here is that there are lots of ways that a business can be inefficient. The idea of the optimise phase is to not only address systems but also look at other ways that the business might be inefficient and deal with those, too.

The following list suggests areas that may offer opportunities to optimise. They are key areas, each followed by some questions to prompt investigations and creative thinking in relation to your own business.

- **Stock level management** How much money is tied up in stock? Can this be reduced? Do stock levels sometimes go too low and cause production to halt?
- **Wasted materials** Do you measure the value of what gets thrown away during production? Are there targets for waste? Could waste be sold instead of being thrown away? (An example is Marmite, which is simply a waste product in brewing.)
- **Lost time** Are there periods in normal operation when employees cannot do anything? How might this time be used in other ways?
- **Repetition** What are the most repeated activities in the business? How much would be saved if each repeat could be substantially reduced?
- **Inefficient processes** What steps could be combined, shortened or eliminated from major business processes to make them more efficient?

■ **Unused facilities** Could your business premises or equipment be put to use in some novel alternative ways?

■ **Biggest spend** What costs the most in the business? Figure this out to home in on opportunities to reduce the spend.

■ **Biggest income** What produces the best sales revenues? How might this be increased or expanded?

This list is not exhaustive, but it does provide a very good place to start. A call centre client was taking messages by writing them on pads and then typing them into a computer system to forward to clients. Upgrading the computer system to eliminate writing on notepads by typing directly into the system improved efficiency by some 60 per cent, providing capacity for real growth without additional staff.

Having reached this Growth Blueprint (19 out of 22), it's likely that you have sufficient personal time to investigate the way in which your business works and find ways to optimise it. So, pick an area that could clearly cost less to run.

Set demanding improvement targets

Once you have chosen a specific system or area to optimise, the secret is to set what seems to be an unattainable target for it. This forces really creative thinking, which produces the best ideas. For example, if you identify that 50 per cent of customer deliveries are late and want to improve on that, immediately set a target of 99 per cent deliveries on time without increasing costs.

Taking this target to a team meeting and asking for ideas on how to achieve it will produce some fascinating input, almost certainly starting with 'There's no way!' right through to ideas that will move you towards it. It is very easy to set a target of shaving 10 per cent off something, but to achieve the step-change improvements that the optimise phase can bring, set targets that are far more stretching.

In motor racing in the 1950s, during a pit stop the driver would get out of his car while mechanics refuelled it and changed the tyres. This normally took several minutes and all the teams behaved in the same way. When Wood Brothers Racing realised that these long pit stops were adding many minutes to the race, they decided to choreograph a far more efficient stop. Immediately, they began to win races, slashing minutes off their normal race times. It would have been easy for them to shave a few seconds off pit stops, but taking them from minutes down to a matter of seconds was the result of setting demanding improvement targets. As we saw earlier, the average F1 pit stop is now around four seconds. Imagine suggesting that to the mechanics in the 1950s – the driver wouldn't have had time to finish his cup of tea.

Try the ideas

Many ideas may seem good on paper but don't work in practice. Find a way to experiment with the ideas without putting your business at risk. It may be that ideas can be tried for real after closing hours or with a special client who is happy to be your guinea pig. No matter what you do, it's important that all except straightforward improvements are properly tested before putting them into routine use.

Implement for real

Once an idea is proven through a trial, the systems can be updated for real and the business will benefit from the improvements. Introduce some kind of measure so that the success of the changes can be confirmed. Afterwards, go back and look for more ways to improve and encourage your team to provide ideas for improvements, too.

Breakthrough Action Plan 19: Optimise your business for efficiency

Here are the steps you need to follow to optimise your business and make it more efficient and profitable.

1 Identify an area or system to optimise.

2 Set a demanding target for any change to achieve.

3 In a team meeting, ask for ideas to optimise and achieve the target.

4 Try out the best ideas until you find a way that will make big improvements.

5 Introduce the change for real, changing systems as required.

6 Measure the effect of the change and let your team know how well it worked.

Key points from this chapter

■ In a smooth, efficient operation, there should be little need for employees to annoy you with minor problems.

■ Asking 'Why?' will enable you to get to the root cause of all problems. Asking 'Who?', however, only promotes a culture of blame and the hiding of real issues.

■ The roadmap to reaching this state is to stabilise the work processes, then lock in procedural systems and, finally, look for improvements through optimisation.

8

Peak service to delight your customers

The Growth Blueprints for outstanding customer service

Do what you do so well that they will want to see it again and bring their friends.
Walt Disney

You may be rather shocked to hear that good service loses customers, but in this chapter you will discover why good service is not good enough and what to do about it. When you deliver customer service that *delights* your customers rather than just leaving them satisfied, magical things start to occur and it directly leads to business growth without any extra marketing. Referrals will increase and you'll find it far easier to win business awards, too. On top of this, your customer retention will go through the roof, while your competitors won't know what you do or how you do it.

A common complaint among people in business is that they have to compete on price, which kills their profit margins. Yet, the reason they are competing on price is that their business offers nothing unique to their customers. If you don't give them some great reasons to buy from you instead of your competitors, you are effectively forcing them to look at price as the only way to choose. Deliver outstanding service and you effectively change the rules of the game, unnerving your competitors and leaving them to scramble for leftovers as your business grows.

You can use the three-layer model of peak service shown in Figure 8.1 as a powerful strategy to distinguish your business from your competition, offering a quality of service that goes beyond simply delivering the goods. When your service delights and surprises your customers, they will become motivated to buy from you again and again. Even better, they will recommend you to their friends. In this way, your service becomes a great marketing tool that will ensure your business has a loyal and enthusiastic customer base to protect you when the economy is down and help you to keep growing. In this chapter you will discover how to build great customer service into the very fabric of your business.

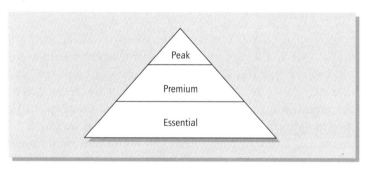

Figure 8.1 The three levels of outstanding customer service

Each of the three levels shown in Figure 8.1 offers higher perceived value of customer service, increasing customer satisfaction, loyalty and, ultimately, referrals. Each level has its own corresponding Growth Blueprint.

Growth Blueprint 20: Essential service for satisfied customers

Too many businesses have inconsistent, disappointing service that seems to say they don't care about customers. Essential service addresses this by systematically fixing the details that can cause disappointment to customers, ensuring they will always receive, at the very least, the service they expect.

One of my clients, who has a restaurant, observed that service is very similar to a house of cards – you have to make sure that the bottom layer is solid before you build on it or the whole thing will collapse. He made this comment after noticing that the glasses on one table were smudged. He immediately checked the other tables and found the same problem everywhere. Rather than shouting at his waiting staff, he invited them to join us at a large table. He then asked them what they would think and how they would feel if presented with glassware that looked like this. It made a powerful point when one of the staff said that, without careful polishing, the glasses looked dirty and it was off-putting to drink from something like that. No matter how wonderful everything else may be, when the basics go wrong, customers will be disappointed.

If you search on YouTube for 'United Breaks Guitars', you will find a video of a bad customer service experience that has had more than 11 million views. The video is by professional musician Dave Carroll and tells how one of his prized guitars was broken while being loaded on to a United Airlines plane by the ground crew. Apparently, after taking his seat on board, he watched in horror through the window as they threw the guitar around.

When he called United to complain afterwards, his complaints were met with complete indifference. Infuriated by the treatment he received, he wrote a song about it. Does it matter if one passenger whinges to a few friends about that airline? Probably not, but this guy recorded a song about his experience and it has been viewed a massive 11 million times on YouTube and United's stock has plummeted! That's the problem with the Internet era – one bad experience can be reported on a review website, shared by people through social networks and it has the potential to cause massive damage to a business. Read on to discover how to gather and use customer experiences as a way to improve.

Gather customer feedback

Consider asking for customer feedback at periodic intervals or after each purchase. A single question, asking what people think of the service, whether good or bad, can provide remarkably helpful information to improve it. It's also worth remembering that, typically, customers will often not complain when they are unhappy with your service, they will just go elsewhere next time. You lose customers and never discover the reasons, which is why asking for feedback is so powerful.

The challenge when running your own business is that you become too close to it. Asking for feedback from customers gives a completely unbiased view that will be honest and helpful in identifying weaknesses and ideas for improvement from the most important perspective of all – that of your customers. Factor the feedback you receive into the changes you make to improve your essential service.

Identify your elements of essential service

So, what are the elements of essential service? It's really all down to one word: expectations. Your service must match the expectations of your customers or they will be dissatisfied. A hotel that offers hot water *most* days will be a disappointment if you stay on a day when there is none.

Use the list of essential service areas given below to assess the service your business delivers and prompt ideas to improve.

- **Environment** What do customers reasonably expect of your business environment? Consider car parking, signage, cleanliness and tidiness. Appearance, sounds and smells are all part of this.
- **Staff appearance** Are your members of staff dressed in a manner consistent with (or better than) what customers would expect?
- **Staff behaviour** Do members of staff treat customers pleasantly? Do they smile, make eye contact, make them feel welcome? Do they treat customers with respect?

■ **Written standards** Are e-mails, letters and text messages well written in correct English?

■ **Phone standards** Are phones answered within three rings? Is there a professional phrase used, such as, 'Thanks for calling L&R Services, this is Lisa speaking, how can I help?'

■ **Quality** Is the product or service up to scratch? Do you have minimum standards that you insist upon and measure in some way?

■ **Delivery** Are products delivered on time, in good condition, every time?

Table 8.1 gives an example of how a restaurant might use a list like this to create a basic plan to improve its essential service.

Table 8.1 Example of an action plan to improve a restaurant's essential service

Essential service areas	Things to do
Environment	Windows polished daily, floors swept after each sitting, tables wiped clear of crumbs and grease, create a bathroom cleanliness checklist
Staff appearance	Uniforms regularly laundered, no elaborate make-up or jewellery, polished shoes
Staff behaviour	Train to greet customers within ten seconds of entry with a smile
Written standards	Spellcheck menus, remove out-of-season dishes from menus
Phone standards	Train staff to always answer with the name of the restaurant
Quality	Food presentation suffers when busy – meet with chef to set minimum standards and brainstorm how to ensure that they are always met
Delivery	Always confirm orders before placing with kitchen to eliminate expensive errors

---

case notes

My first car was a Peugeot and was serviced regularly by the town's dealer. On collection, I would invariably find a strong smell of oil inside the car and both the steering wheel and gear knob would be greasy from the mechanic's hands. The garage also had a tiny car park and the cars were tightly packed in next to each other. When I asked someone to get mine out for me I was laughed at and told that I could manage. I was an inexperienced driver and found it deeply unnerving to extract my car carefully without knocking into any of the surrounding vehicles. Needless to say, I have never bought another car from this dealer.

I never told the staff that I was dissatisfied – I just showed it through my actions, never again buying a car from that garage and choosing to have it serviced elsewhere. Its service was simply unsatisfactory and cost that dealer a customer for life. I have often wondered how many more customers the dealer lost for the same reasons.

Use systems to consistently deliver essential service

The list in Table 8.1 could easily be turned into a series of simple systems, with checklists, whiteboards and similar, all playing a role in making the essential service consistent and ensuring customer satisfaction. For help with creating checklists and systems, see Chapter 7.

Systems are at the heart of consistency. When the elements of your customer service are integrated with the systems that run your business, the customers will receive exactly the same service, time and time again. Consistency will get customers coming back repeatedly. Fast food chain McDonald's has completely systemised the way that it runs its restaurants – from the menus, the way the food is cooked and even the words members of staff say when serving you. Its systems ensure that customers receive the same level of service every time, from every store.

Success tip

In a study at the John Hunter Hospital in Australia, people were seen to have greater confidence in doctors who dressed smartly than in those who dressed casually (and if the doctor wore a nose ring, confidence plummeted completely!) While patients are not qualified to evaluate a doctor's clinical ability, they go by what they see – a doctor in a shirt and tie with a white coat will give them more confidence than one wearing jeans. Choose uniforms and dress codes based on what you want customers to think.

Breakthrough Action Plan 20: Essential service for satisfied customers

Follow these steps to deliver the essential service that ensures satisfied customers, time after time.

1 Read the list of essential service areas earlier in this chapter to identify ways in which your business may be disappointing customers and leaving them dissatisfied.

2 Gather customer feedback to increase your knowledge of where there may be problems with your service.

3 Formulate your plan to improve your essential service (like the example given for a restaurant).

4 Improve the operation of your business to deliver essential service consistently using the techniques described in Chapter 7.

Growth Blueprint 21: Premium service creates customer loyalty

Your business must be delivering essential service before you move on to this next level. Fundamental problems will cause customers to be disappointed and walk away, never to return. It would be like a restaurant putting a beautiful flower arrangement on to a greasy table – the flowers do not make up for basic problems with service.

At the next level, creating a sense of something special for your customers will encourage customer loyalty, which is critical to fend off competitors' attempts to lure them away from you. The delivery of a premium service that pampers customers is one of the strongest defences you can build around your client base. Of course, a premium service also adds value, so permits higher pricing; indeed, people often expect to pay more for a premium service and so this works in your favour.

The essential service stage is just that – about the bare essentials of your service. Now you need to add a layer of finesse for your customers to feel totally loved by your business. How you achieve this can be tricky, because every industry has its own little secrets that you must crack in order to be a cut above the ordinary.

The psychology of customers

When a new customer rang optician Richard explaining that a part of his designer glasses had split and fallen off from wear and tear, Richard offered to post him a new part, completely free of charge. The customer had not bought the glasses from Richard in the first place and was astonished at this offer. A month later, the customer visited the practice in person and placed an order worth in excess of £1000. This is just one of many orders produced as a direct result of premium service – that is, delivering more than the customer expects.

Because most businesses provide a fairly mediocre service, customers tend to set low expectations of them. Doing something extraordinary, like Richard did, will make a lasting impression. Build several things like this into your service that demonstrate the same attention to the customer relationship and the overall customer experience will be transformed into something very special. This, then, is how you build premium service into your business.

Success tip

A truly premium service – like that offered by the optician mentioned earlier – creates the possibility of premium pricing. Just like flying with a major airline, in economy there are no frills, while business class has more legroom, bigger seats and better service. It also makes a lot more profit than the rest of the plane by charging more than twice the price of a standard ticket. If you introduce a better quality of service, you create the option to increase profits substantially by taking your business upmarket to sell to more affluent customers.

Ten ways to deliver more than customers expect

Every industry will have its own unique touches that are practised by the best of the businesses that operate within it. The challenge is to figure out what those special touches are for your specific industry. Go to a top restaurant, for example, and every member of staff you look at will respond with eye contact and a friendly smile. You will be taken to your table and your chair gently pushed in very slightly as you sit down – sometimes called 'the magic touch' by restauranteurs.

Here are ten ways to deliver more than customers expect.

- **Don't make customers wait** respect your customers' time – they are choosing to buy from you.
- **Be helpful, even when it makes you no profit** if a customer is confused or stuck, be helpful and generous with advice, even when there is no likely sale in it. They will remember you.
- **Overdeliver** offer to take their bags to the car, offer to gift wrap their purchase, offer them a seat if they look tired – think bigger than the transaction.
- **Give extra value** surprise customers with little gifts or bonus items with their purchases. A friend treasures a miniature hard hat given to him by a supplier 20 years ago!

▪ **Make customers feel important** remember their names when you speak to them. A great bartender can apparently remember 3000 names and the drink each person prefers. Train your staff to 'treat them like royalty to earn their loyalty!'

▪ **Use their names** there is no sweeter sound than your own name said with respect. Say the customers' names when you speak to them to help them feel closer to you. Consider the type of relationship you have with your customers, too – so, a tailor's shop might address John Smith as Mr Smith, whereas a trendy young boutique might call him John.

▪ **Send a 'thank you' card** after a big purchase, send the client a card to say 'Thanks!' We are thanked so rarely for our custom it can make a huge impact.

▪ **Make eye contact and smile** as described earlier, top restaurants do this to help customers feel that they are in friendly surroundings. When all of your staff do this, you create an incredibly welcoming atmosphere.

▪ **Regular communication** if your transactions take a long time to complete – like a loan application or a business sales agent – communicate every few days. Even if there's nothing new to report, it lets them know that everything is still OK and there's nothing to worry about.

▪ **Use competitors for inspiration** monitor trade press for ideas, visit or buy from companies with the best reputations in your industry. What do they do that is special or different? Take careful notes and brainstorm ideas for your business.

---

case notes

A mortgage broker client set a goal of offering the best customer service in the industry. Since mortgage applications typically take three weeks to process and the stress of buying a house can be significant, the clients would be given an update by e-mail or on the phone every two days, even when there was nothing to report.

In addition to communicating effectively during the transaction, customers are remembered afterwards, too. A customer feedback letter is sent a week after their mortgage has been approved. The broker sends a 'New home!' card when the mortgage is for a new property, sending out birthday and Christmas cards, too. These regular little touches result in fabulous feedback, great customer retention and better than average referrals, too.

Build the systems and train your staff

When you have identified your premium service ideas, it's time to build the systems required to support them (see Chapter 7) and then train your staff to stick to them. Educating members of staff about the subtleties involved in premium service is challenging because some of it may be difficult for them – some people don't naturally feel comfortable making frequent eye contact, for example. You must encourage them to stick at it.

Many business owners simply don't want to go through the pain of educating their staff to work like this and settle for second best instead. Yet, when you insist on high standards, after a while, a bit of magic occurs when your members of staff suddenly realise what they have created and become very proud of the service they provide, maintaining your standards even when you are not there.

It is important that staff follow the systems 100 per cent of the time. A shop assistant who serves 280 people in a shift and is pleasant to 279 of them will think that he or she has done a great job. The one person that assistant snapped at, however, only had *one* experience of the shop that day – and it was a bad one. That customer might just tell a friend about the terrible treatment received and a bad reputation spreads like wildfire.

Success tip

I have come across several businesses that have installed phone systems to filter incoming calls, advising callers to 'Press 1 if you want to speak to sales, 2 for administration' and so on. The companies that installed them thought they sounded more professional than picking the phone up directly, but how many times have you called a business and felt *pleased* to hear an automated system like this? If *you* don't like it, your *customers* won't either. Avoid these unless you absolutely require them.

Breakthrough Action Plan 21: Premium service creates customer loyalty

Follow the steps below to deliver a premium service to create customer loyalty – but only after you have fixed your essential service!

1 Decide whether or not you will be taking your service upmarket to a premium service level to determine how far beyond essential service the changes will need to go.

2 Using the list of ten ways to deliver more than customers expect earlier in this chapter, prepare an action plan to create a premium service.

3 Build the systems and obtain any additional resources required to deliver a premium service.

4 Train your members of staff and work to 'indoctrinate' them with why their 100 per cent participation is so important.

Growth Blueprint 22: Peak service produces customer referrals

The idea of peak service is to create something that people will tell their friends about. With businesses being increasingly competitive and the ease with which your customers can search for alternatives on the Internet, it's more important than ever that you find ways to make your business more memorable than any other. You can achieve this by adding surprises to your service that will delight your customers so much they will tell stories about you! These are high points because they are at the very peak of customer service and cannot easily be surpassed.

Some friends travel every year to the same hotel in the tropics, using the same travel agent. They have used this same agent for ten years now and their loyalty is a result of the great service they receive every time. The peak service they receive includes a gift within a day or two of returning home. One time it was a pack of scented candles and a wooden holder, beautifully presented in a smart box wrapped with a ribbon. We often chat about holidays and, without fail, they will mention the name of their travel agent as part of the conversation. They are so pleased with the service that they want everybody else to know, too.

Just think for a moment about the value created by this travel agent's peak service. Over ten years, this couple has spent tens of thousands of pounds and the travel agent has not had to spend anything substantial to advertise. The cost of the candles is small change compared to the profit on these holidays. It doesn't matter if they charge a few pounds more for the holiday overall, the experience that they sell takes them beyond pure price comparisons because they sell a luxury holiday experience. They will certainly be doing the same for all other customers, so they will be capturing new customers and rarely losing them. If this can work in an industry as competitive and Internet-based as travel has become in recent years, just imagine how much it could do for your business, too. Look after your great customers and surprise them from time to time with peak service and they will look after your business in return.

Now we return to our example of a restaurant. What sorts of things can it do to deliver some especially memorable moments for its customers, to get them telling their friends about the experience they've had? One simple, elegant and yet inexpensive idea is to give out a recipe card for a particularly special dish, like a favourite sweet or starter, for people to try making for themselves at home. Not only does this mean that they will be reminded of your restaurant when they make it but also they will probably be serving it to friends, too. Just imagine the conversation: 'OK, so it didn't work out too great here, but you should try it at The Golden Goose – it's simply brilliant. Shall we book a table for next Saturday night?'

---

case notes

Just outside Congleton in Cheshire is a restaurant called Pecks, which describes its special dining experience as a 'Theatre of Food'. Patrons are seated by eight o'clock, when the smartly dressed waiting staff parade through with sample dishes of each starter on the menu. Waiters stop at every table to describe the dishes in mouthwatering detail. This show is repeated for each course. The restaurant has trained its staff to deliver service in a remarkable way.

For little additional cost, the owners have turned dining at Pecks into an extraordinary experience and the word of mouth marketing it creates means that bookings need to be made months in advance. The grand finale for the evening is the choice of up to four different desserts in half-portions – a fitting end to a perfect dinner.

This, then, is a spectacular example of what is meant by peak service. The experience transforms it from a *good* meal into something you will talk about for weeks afterwards. Note, though, that this would not have worked if the food had not been up to scratch; it would not have worked if the place had been scruffy and worn out.

Peak service will be very different for different businesses. While Pecks is an example of grand thinking, there are many things that are simple but feasible for any creative business owner to use. Below is a list of some examples for a range of businesses, each designed to add a little character to the business and make it memorable and worth telling friends about.

- **Car dealership** install a Scalextric track for kids to play with while their parents talk. Run a monthly client challenge race with silly prizes to encourage them to come in more often, too.

- **Antiques shop** run an annual customer sale in the style of a period party for clients, with prizes for the best costumes and old-fashioned cakes and treats on offer.

- **Accountancy practice** replace the series of standard reminder letters with customised greeting cards that amuse and remind all at once.

- **Restaurant** employ a guitar-playing waiter to serenade couples in a subtle way during their main course.

- **Taxi business** provide complementary mints to customers and offer bottled water for sale in the taxi. While not free, this would be welcomed by many passengers, as well as making a little extra profit.

- **Plumber** give customers an emergency kit – a neat bag of instructions about what to do in a plumbing emergency, printed with the plumber's emergency and normal contact numbers.

- **Grocers** drop an extra piece of ripe fruit into a bag after it has been weighed to make a delightful surprise when customers open their shopping when they arrive home. Since the fruit is ripe, it's only what the grocer would be throwing away in two days' time anyway.

- **Dental practice** when Dr Paddi Lund created his 'happiness-centred business', one of many things he did was to install a round oven in his practice that produced freshly baked, low-sugar biscuits and cakes. It became an incredible talking point for his customers.

Success tip

Peak service is about surprise, not cost. The simplest ideas, when unusual and unexpected, can turn into fun stories for your customers to tell their friends about. Look for examples of the unusual from businesses you use – especially the small businesses to which you are loyal. What is special about them?

Breakthrough Action Plan 22: Peak service produces customer referrals

This is perhaps the most challenging action plan in the book, because it requires true creative thinking.

1 Grab a blank pad of paper and some pens.

2 Set a timer to go off in ten minutes and spend the full time brainstorming peak service ideas. Don't stop until the ten minutes are up – even if you feel like you've run out of ideas.

3 Discuss the best ideas with your team members, asking them for their ideas, too.

4 Decide what to do, then do it!

5 Introduce your peak service ideas and listen for comments and thoughts. Keep what works; eliminate what doesn't.

Key points from this chapter

■ Essential service is only delivered when you have robust systems and every employee achieving the standards that you require. This is a foundation on which business growth is built.

■ Essential service provides a sound business and keeps you trading successfully, *but* loyalty will only follow if you offer premium service. This is worth repeating: don't introduce premium service until essential service is in place and delivering customer satisfaction.

■ You can help customers to produce referrals for you by giving them some fun experiences that make them say, 'Wow!' and tell their friends, too. This is peak service.

9

How other businesses have used these techniques to double their business

Stories about businesses to inspire you

Two roads diverged in a wood, and I,
I took the one less traveled by,
And that has made all the difference.
Robert Frost, 'The Road Not Taken'

This chapter presents five case studies drawn from my experience of helping businesses apply the Growth Blueprints to improve their situations drastically. My approach has always been exactly as set out in this book:

- Identify the biggest Barrier to Growth (you can do this by answering the questions in Chapter 1).

- Address the Barrier using the corresponding Growth Blueprint.

- Find and address the next Barrier to Growth.

Each of the stories here summarises many months of work and some tough decisions that had to be made to deliver extraordinary results. While they may sometimes seem straightforward, the benefit of hindsight always makes it appear far simpler than it was in practice – success rarely happens easily or overnight.

The Riverside Restaurant

www.riverside-restaurant.co.uk

The twice-cooked beef I ordered for dinner that Tuesday night was one of most succulently delicious things I have ever eaten. So why was there only one other table occupied in this outstanding restaurant? Business was so slow that by 10 p.m. the owner and chef, Andrew Rowbotham, was able to join me at my table to talk about his business.

Driven by his passion for sourcing the best local ingredients and beautifully cooked food, Andrew had opened the restaurant a couple of years previously. On weekend evenings the restaurant was full of appreciative diners. As this evening demonstrated, however, wonderful food was not enough to put bums on seats during the week and Andrew was in the unenviable position of finding that his successful Friday and Saturday nights were subsidising the losses he made during the week.

As we sat drinking our glasses of Rioja, Andrew told me more about his business and passion. The restaurant is situated in the quiet town of Barnard Castle (near Durham). It's not a wealthy or large area, having a population of only 6000. Its true wealth lies in the majestic River Tees that flows right past the restaurant and in the surrounding hilly woodlands, which attract tourists throughout the year.

Andrew developed the idea of opening his own restaurant while managing a steak restaurant for somebody else in Spain. Returning home, he persuaded his family to provide him with financial backing and he opened up the restaurant. He visited local farms and butchers to find the best local produce and created a menu of traditional dishes with a modern twist. The restaurant was dressed to look like a fine-quality bistro and his wine list matched the quality of his foods.

Andrew expected that word would soon spread about his wonderful creations. Despite a great deal of marketing effort, nothing seemed to be working and the restaurant's patronage had plateaued. He knew that his website was poor, but the newspaper and radio exposure he had achieved were exceptional for such a small business. Sadly, these alone were not delivering more customers.

Reflecting on what the problems might be, Andrew thought, 'Maybe it's the recession? Maybe the town is too small? Perhaps the menu is too expensive or fancy for this area?' 'What can we do', he wondered, 'to fill these difficult, quiet midweek evenings?'

We began with a series of questions similar to those in Chapter 1 and this took us to a fundamental Barrier to Growth: Andrew didn't have a customer database that could be used for target marketing. On the back of a napkin, I sketched out a simple feedback form, similar to the one shown in Figure 9.1.

Thanks for dining with us. We aim to provide the best dining experience in town. Please let us know how we did tonight for you – tell us and we'll enter you into our monthly draw to win a free meal for two.			
First name:		E-mail address:	
Last name:		Mobile phone:	
Address:			
Your comments			
Tick this box to receive offers and special deals (including £5 off next time)			☐

Figure 9.1 Simple feedback form for data capture

This took us literally five minutes to draft. At the time, Andrew looked at me as if to say, 'Is that it? Is that going to double my business?' Well, it might look simple, but this form was going to become *strategically* very important.

Offering the customer a chance to win something gave them an incentive to give us their contact details and their immediate permission to keep them informed; they had entered the marketing loop.

Over the next weeks, as a nice touch, Andrew took the bill to each table personally and invited the diners to enter the draw. Stomachs filled and rosy cheeked, the diners were quite happy to fill out their details.

That was easy.

The next thing to look at was how effective his various advertising methods were. We put in place a tally sheet, like those explained in Chapter 5. The customer feedback form and this tally sheet required data to be collected for several weeks, so we returned to the Barriers to Growth questions and began an in-depth look at Andrew's profit margins.

We carefully reviewed the menu to eliminate a series of inconsistencies. For example, the most expensive steak meals were far less profitable than the midrange meals – we fixed that quickly! Andrew commented to me that, despite being right under his nose, he had never noticed what was happening here – a common challenge when hands-on people are running their businesses themselves.

He was also missing a huge opportunity to make The Riverside Restaurant stand out as a really special dining experience. As mentioned, when we first met Andrew had told me of his passion for sourcing only the finest local ingredients, but he was not making this known to his customers. People who enjoy good food also enjoy the feeling of inclusion in the selection of truly wonderful ingredients from the area. It turns a simple steak supper into a story they can tell their friends and gives them a sense of well-being, supporting local farmers.

So, we redesigned the menu to include a statement of Andrew's personal philosophy about local produce and how he had built up a relationship with specific farmers. Individual items were renamed to reinforce this – 'Twice-cooked "Mount Grace Farm" Beef Steak' speaks volumes about the source of the meat and appropriately positions it as a special dish.

While all of this was happening, we collected the tally sheets so that we could have a detailed look at the marketing activity. When we analysed the results, it was clear that the marketing was having a very limited effect. Andrew was confident that the local papers were very popular, so we agreed to rewrite his ads using the AIDA method outlined in Chapter 5. An offer was made for midweek diners, to encourage people to come and try the restaurant for the first time, and the impact was immediate.

Then, thanks to his welcoming, friendly approach to customers and his fanatical attention to detail over food and service, Andrew's request for their contact details quickly skyrocketed his customer database numbers to over 1000 names. When he kept in touch with them via e-mail to entice them back, monthly sales went up by over 60 per cent.

Returning again to the Barriers to Growth we found that the extra pressure that came with the increased volumes of customers in the restaurant highlighted something Andrew had sensed for some time. One team member was just not cut out for this type of fine dining experience. Efforts to train the person failed, so they parted company.

Andrew continues to ring frequently to tell me about a record-breaking week or how changes in prices have been accepted without question by his customers. He has more than doubled his business and is justifiably proud of this achievement.

When I asked for his permission to use his story as a case study in this book Andrew told me about something else that had happened. One Friday morning, as sometimes happens with restaurants, he found that, inexplicably, there was only one booking for that evening. Immediately, he sent 250 text messages to people in his marketing loop, offering them a 'deal', and, by mid-afternoon, every table was filled.

With The Riverside Restaurant now successfully established, Andrew is developing a new gastropub with guest rooms, which I'm looking forward to visiting.

The Riverside Restaurant used the following Growth Blueprints:

- Lead capture marketing (Chapter 5)
- Robust profit margins (Chapter 3)
- Make your business stand out (Chapter 5)
- Magnetise your marketing (Chapter 5)
- Top ten marketing channels (Chapter 5)
- Right people (Chapter 4)
- Premium service (Chapter 8)

Zoom Answer Call, Telephone Answering Service

www.zoomuk.co.uk

When Chella Heyes first started her telephone answering service, she wanted to be her own boss and, within just a few years, had built a thriving small business. Then the twins arrived! Although Chella was able to balance her time between babies and the business, the inevitable drain on her mojo left her feeling, in her own words, 'asleep at the wheel'. She had lost sight of her original dream – a business that she loved to run, her team loved being a part of, and her customers loved, too. The first stage, when she looked at the Barriers to Growth, was energising her business mojo by revisiting her original vision, which required some tweaking due to the needs of her young family. This process didn't take long – she described it as her 'wake-up call'.

Looking again at her Barriers to Growth, the next thing required was a change to the structure of her business to introduce extra management help. Thus, all the essential work for the business could continue regardless of whether Chella was present or not. She promoted and trained some telephone operators and recruited replacements for them. Chella's working hours halved instantly and this freed her mind to be able to focus on developing her business.

To push the business to a higher level of performance, Chella began a complete reworking of the daily operations, creating her operations manual.

The final step to doubling her business was increasing the profits by looking for a step-change in efficiency that came about by optimising the way the business handled calls. A new computerised system was introduced that cut the average customer call time from five minutes to three minutes, providing a massive increase in capacity. A spin-off benefit from this retraining was that training time for new staff was cut from two weeks to three days.

A nice twist to the story is that Chella's business doubled while her involvement halved!

Zoom Answer Call used the following Growth Blueprints

- Get your mojo back! (Chapter 2)
- Right people (Chapter 4)
- Systemise to create your operations manual (Chapter 7)
- Optimise your business for efficiency (Chapter 7)

Superwarm Services, Central Heating Systems

www.superwarm.co.uk

John Carmichael realised that he needed to do something dramatically different if his Edinburgh-based central heating systems business was to remain strong. The recession was taking its toll on the building trades, people he had known for years were hinting at closure and news headlines offered a continuous diatribe of doom and gloom.

Doing his best to fight back, John used the traditional tactics he could see his competitors also using – putting more funds towards bigger and more frequent ads, and updating his website. He had minor success with Google's Adwords' pay per click service. When leads came, he fought to win work by offering aggressive discounts.

Still, where there should have been bookings, his diary remained sparse and the thrill of being in business was replaced with fear for what the future might hold. After laying off staff, he sat tight and hoped that the economy would pick up a bit. Then, at the start of a new year, John decided it was time to get some fresh eyes on his business and he contacted me.

We considered his Barriers to Growth and decided to focus on his sales, marketing and service processes. John had already created a culture of strong customer service, which he formalised by introducing his 'Ten Commandments of Super Service' as part of his one-page growth plan.

John Carmichael's Ten Commandments of Super Service

1 **Always keep your house secure**
We will not leave your key under the plant pot and we will lock the door so your home is kept safe at all times.

2 **Always use dust sheets**
We will cover and protect your carpets and furniture from dust and footprints.

3 **Always patch up holes**
Any holes created through your walls will be patched and sealed to prevent drafts and dampness.

4 **Always sweep and clean up**
We will tidy up behind ourselves, leaving your home pristine and ready for your return.

5 **Always provide comprehensive guarantee**
So you don't have to worry about technical glitches, everything is covered.

6 **Always be on time**
We will turn up when we say and do the job on time, so you can get on with what's important to you.

7 **Always communicate with you**
Keeping you informed of how things are progressing so you can manage your day.

8 **Always give you a fixed price quote**
So there are no hidden surprises and the job comes in to your budget, every time.

9 **Only turn off water and heating when absolutely necessary**
So you will be without facilities for the minimum amount of time.

10 **Never ask for a penny until the job is complete**
To give you peace of mind that the job will be done to your complete satisfaction.

Some advertising was generating leads, although we measured that less than one in three of these were converted into sales. Introducing the 4-step sales process and rewriting his quotations using a variation on the AIDA principles very quickly turned this up to 50 per cent. John was astounded!

Next, we added in some carefully targeted marketing, aimed at specific customers using direct mail and Internet strategies. Simultaneously, we did a detailed review of John's prices. His quality of service was undeniably 'premium' and so – despite a recession – we increased his prices accordingly.

Now, even in tough times, the business is expanding, his fleet of vehicles is steadily being upgraded and he is employing new engineers. The order book is full for six weeks ahead and John is excited and bullish about the future.

Within six months of working together, Superwarm Services' sales had risen 98 per cent – another business doubled.

Superwarm Services used the following Growth Blueprints:

◼ Create high-performance salespeople (Chapter 6)

◼ Lead capture marketing (Chapter 5)

◼ Premium service creates customer loyalty (Chapter 8)

◼ Robust profit margins (Chapter 3)

◼ Make your business stand out (Chapter 5)

◼ Magnetise your marketing (Chapter 5)

Mrs X's property management business

Sometimes the challenges a business faces seem embarrassingly simple with hindsight. In this case, Mrs X was not keen to have the story about her business linked to her name. I wanted to include her story, however, as it shows some very different Barriers to Growth from those described in the earlier stories, so, to respect her wishes I have made it anonymous.

Mrs X was introduced to me by her accountant. I was told that her team had no respect for her, she was frustrated and the business was getting nowhere fast, despite being very busy.

At our first meeting, Mrs X told me that she wanted to make the business more profitable and grow it substantially from the 87 properties she was currently managing to at least 200. In the first couple of hours of our meeting, we were interrupted by a series of issues related to a tenant or property.

As it was our first meeting, I carefully observed both the frequency of interruptions and the incredibly simple questions that her staff brought to her. Exasperated after the fourth or fifth interruption, she shouted, 'Leave me alone, can't you see I'm busy? Nobody is to disturb me again!' and slammed her door shut.

With tears welling up in her eyes, she told me that she felt close to breaking point because her staff could do nothing without her. She was losing sleep and overeating, her 16-year-old son was just starting his A-levels and she felt like she hardly knew him any more, because she spent so little quality time with him.

To get a better understanding of her Barriers to Growth, we took a look at some key facts relating to her business. First, her lead generation was off the scale – hundreds of enquiries came in every month from potential tenants, yet sales were very poor, with less than one in ten resulting in a successful sale.

The next obvious issue was a pile of property maintenance problems reported by tenants that were not being efficiently addressed, with the result that time was being wasted making excuses to tenants rather than getting the work done. Finally, Mrs X explained that landlords often complained for one of two reasons: rent was not collected efficiently and new properties could sit vacant for months after being taken on by her business.

She finished by saying that her staff seemed to pay little attention to what she asked them to do and nobody seemed to care about the business like she did. In short, she knew that, without some drastic changes, her business was stuck and would either stay there forever or slide backwards as she lost enthusiasm for it.

At first glance, a business with so many pressing issues can seem like a really badly knotted ball of string. So, you just have to find one end and start the untangling until it gradually becomes useful to you again. There was clearly a great deal of potential in Mrs X's business, with strong lead generation providing the fuel for growth, if we could just get the operations firing on all cylinders. We needed to create order out of chaos, stop all the busywork and become a lot more productive.

Out of all this tangled mess, we found that the first real Barrier to Growth was a lack of organisation. The business had grown fast and nobody knew what their real jobs were. This exercise revealed that Mrs X's employees, in shopfront desks, were all expected to handle a prodigious volume of leads each day, take potential tenants to view properties and also share responsibility for scheduling various trades to sort out maintenance issues.

We quickly drew up a new organisation chart for her business and sketched out what roles were needed to make the business function more effectively, without Mrs X's input every five minutes. Figure 9.2 shows the initial organisation chart we sketched out together.

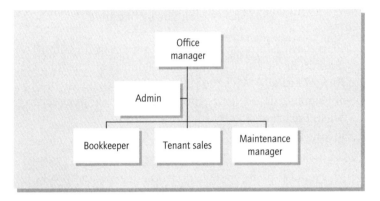

Figure 9.2

Here's a thumbnail description of each of the jobs you can see in the chart in Figure 9.2.

- Office manager (Mrs X)
  - Looks after landlords and ensures that their needs are met.
  - Takes care of marketing for new landlords, new properties and new tenants.
  - Maintains an overview of all key processes to ensure that customers are properly cared for with premium service.
- Bookkeeper
  - Manages financial paperwork in accordance with legal requirements.
  - Produces management accounts that enable Mrs X to manage the business.
  - Chases rent payments and ensures that landlords receive their rent on time.

- Tenant sales
  - Handles incoming enquiries about properties.
  - Arranges and carries out viewings with potential tenants.
  - Alerts the maintenance manager regarding maintenance issues reported by tenants or identified in property visits.
  - Increases the value of each sale by upselling.
- Maintenance manager
  - Keeps a master list of all property issues.
  - Gains approval for works from landlords.
  - Resolves urgent issues affecting health, safety or property security immediately.
  - Provides report each week to the office manager on maintenance activities.
  - Produces profit by subcontracting maintenance works.
- Admin
  - Provides general admin support to the office manager.
  - Collates weekly report covering maintenance, finance and sales in time for the weekly meeting.
  - Manages the take-on of new properties and allocates work as appropriate for gas checks, etc.

These details were sufficient for Mrs X to realise that, by allocating clear job descriptions to every employee, there would be no confusion about responsibilities and it would be easier to train staff to do one job really well, than expect them all to do lots of different tasks with no clear responsibility for any of them.

After doing this, we held a team meeting and explained to everybody that change was coming. The new organisation chart was drawn on a flipchart and Mrs X explained how each job worked.

After solving the organisational issues, Mrs X explained that some landlords were getting angry about having placed properties with her that had no tenants after several months. The administrator was out of her depth trying to solve this on her own, so she got a whiteboard and drew up a chart like the one shown in Chapter 7, in the section on systemisation.

For each new property, every single step in the process to getting it rented out was tracked by recording it on a board, including ensuring that there are safety certificates for gas boilers, an inventory of the contents of the property, getting photos of properties to use in ads, placing the ads on various websites, taking deposits from tenants and so on. The administrator now updates the board every evening and a meeting is held each morning to review progress with the whole team.

A target was set to get each property on the market within five working days of it being taken on and the administrator highlights each time this has failed to happen. While Mrs X runs the meetings, it is the administrator who provides the facts to show what is happening. This daily focus on new property take-on quickly brought the previous problems in this area under control.

Finally, we addressed the maintenance challenge by starting to use a computer system that Mrs X had purchased a year previously but had had no time to put into practice. This system has a record for each property owned by a landlord and includes a maintenance module to track any issues and their resolution. Properties were entered into the system by the administrator to bring it up to date.

Salespeople now enter maintenance issues into the system and the maintenance manager then prioritises and updates each job as it is done. A standing agenda item to review maintenance was added to the daily meetings and the administrator now uses the system to report on progress and jobs that appear to be overdue.

These daily meetings produce a simple action plan, with the majority of actions owned by employees instead of Mrs X. A side-benefit stemming from the computer system is the exceptional level of reporting it gives to landlords. Each landlord has access to his or her portfolio online and can look at the performance and maintenance of each property. This has increased loyalty as no other local agents provide information to this high standard.

After stabilising and systemising the business, Mrs X was concerned that profit was still not sufficiently strong. We reviewed the management accounts and discovered that some properties and landlords were consuming a lot of time and effort, while making very little real profit.

By speaking to the landlords, several were 'sacked' as customers and others were asked to pay a slightly higher premium for the service. Thanks to the great service they are now providing, this went down without a problem.

Meanwhile, the members of the sales team were asked to sell additional services to tenants from a list the team brainstormed in one of their meetings. This substantially improved margins. We then put in place a sales forecast and budget for the business that formed the basis for sales targets and cut spending on frivolous and unnecessary items.

If you were to speak now to Mrs X, she would not easily admit the challenges she once faced. Her business has more than doubled, she has over 250 properties, there is far more profit and she has managed to develop a stronger relationship with her son. She is also confident that her business will continue to grow without her ever losing control again.

Mrs X used the following Growth Blueprints:

- Right people (Chapter 4)
- Stabilise to eliminate firefighting (Chapter 7)
- Properly managed cash flow (Chapter 3)
- Robust profit margins (Chapter 3)
- Realistic sales forecast and budget (Chapter 3)
- Essential service for satisfied customers (Chapter 8)
- Premium service creates customer loyalty (Chapter 8)
- Systemise to create your operations manual (Chapter 7)
- Optimise your business for efficiency (Chapter 7)

Airworld Tours

www.airworldtours.co.uk

The directors of Airworld Tours, a luxury travel business, were deeply concerned that their hard work to build a multimillion pound travel business over ten years would be unravelled by a 'perfect storm' of problems hitting them all at the same time.

Jamal Shahid and Mohammad Akram started luxury tour operator Airworld Tours Limited in the 1990s. Using consistent advertising on TV's Teletext Holidays service, they quickly grew the business until they had achieved annual sales in the millions. So far so good. Then, after a decade of profitable growth, that storm hit them:

- the switchover from analogue to digital TV destroyed their major source of leads, which left them with barely half the leads they needed to keep the business operating successfully

- the banking crisis hit consumer confidence and they saw competitor firms falling by the wayside, thanks to tighter margins from airlines and hotels, added to smaller numbers of holidaymakers

- the pound weakened tremendously against the major currencies of their most popular destinations, with European holidays especially becoming prohibitively expensive.

The directors of the business scrabbled around for ideas that could save them. They invested thousands in pay per click marketing to generate more website traffic, they sent out thousands of leaflets, placed ads with major newspapers and continued to produce their beautiful, 100+ page travel brochure. Yet, despite their best efforts, sales slumped horribly by 30 per cent on their previous best year, which began to feel like a distant memory instead of their recent history.

When I came on the scene, as always, I did an audit of the Barriers to Growth they were facing and quickly realised that the first priority was more efficient sales activity management. As a matter of urgency, the sales team needed some support, training and guidelines to ensure every opportunity that came in was maximised, with more leads becoming more sales.

We introduced an effective customer relationship management (CRM) system to monitor the quality and volume of leads from each source. The staff used an online booking system the company had produced itself, so this was updated to store history and action information for each client and booking, providing a powerful tool for monitoring, managing and reporting sales performance. Simultaneously, the four-step sales process (see Chapter 6) was rolled out and the salespeople were monitored to ensure that the new methods were being adhered to.

With the sales function getting on track, I moved on to the next barrier. Airworld needed to develop a niche marketing strategy so that lead generation could focus on its most highly profitable types of holidays. This focus was scary for the directors and their team at first, as it meant putting a disproportionate amount of their marketing effort and investment into a relatively small niche type of holiday. We had a long discussion about this, debating the benefits of dropping many of their long-term ideas and experiences of marketing and instead concentrating on a smaller number of destinations. Finally, after much debate, I persuaded them that it was the right thing to do.

The most serious challenge was to find a new marketing channel for them to replace Teletext, but this proved easier than expected. A combination of several Internet marketing strategies (including online lead capture, Adwords and search engine optimisation, amongst other ideas) came together to produce a very strong new source of leads.

The owners worked intensively on their business for almost 12 months to get all of this done. Because of their focus on making changes, there was a feeling that progress was very slow. This changed when a chance updating of their neglected sales figures showed truly explosive growth of 89 per cent over their performance the previous year. This was the fastest growth they had ever experienced in a single year and left both Jamal and Mohammad delighted to have really turned a corner.

After just one year, their sales had doubled to higher levels than before their 'perfect storm' hit, with millions being added to their sales. Their goals now are to grow the business to at least four times its original size.

Airworld used the following Growth Blueprints:

- Sales activity management (Chapter 6)
- Create high-performance salespeople (Chapter 6)
- Lead capture marketing (Chapter 5)
- Premium service (Chapter 8)
- Make your business stand out (Chapter 5)
- Top ten marketing channels (Chapter 5)

Further reading

Bannatyne, D. (2007) *Anyone Can Do It: From an ice cream van to Dragon's Den*. Orion.

Barrow, C. and Tracy, J. A. (2004) *Understanding Business Accounting for Dummies (UK Edition): A reference for the rest of us!* John Wiley & Sons.

Beckwith, H. (2001) *Selling the Invisible: A field guide to modern marketing*. Texere Publishing.

Blanchard, K. and Johnson, S. (1994) *The One Minute Manager*. HarperCollins.

Branson, R. (2010) *Screw It, Let's Do It: Lessons in life*. Virgin.

Callahan, S. (1996) *Adrift: Seventy-six days lost at sea*. Ballantine.

Carpenter, S. (2009) *Work the System: The simple mechanics of making more and working less*. Greenleaf.

Christensen, J., Lundin, S. C. and Paul, H. (2002) *Fish!: A remarkable way to boost morale and improve results*. Hodder.

Cialdini, R. B. (2007) *Influence: The psychology of persuasion*. HarperBusiness.

Covey, S. R. (2004) *The 7 Habits of Highly Effective People: Powerful lessons in personal change*. Free Press.

Dennis, F. (2007) *How to Get Rich: The distilled wisdom of one of Britain's wealthiest self-made entrepreneurs*. Ebury.

Dyson, J. (2000) *Against the Odds: An autobiography* (2nd edn). Texere Publishing.

Freese, T. A. (2001) *Secrets of Question Based Selling: How the most powerful tool in business can double your sales results*. Sourcebooks, Inc.

Godin, Seth (2009) *Purple Cow: Transform your business by being remarkable*. Portfolio.

Hill, N. (2008) *Think and Grow Rich*. Wilder.

Hopkins, C. C. (2010) *Scientific Advertising*. Eigal Meirovich.

King, B. (2010) *How to Double Your Sales: The ultimate masterclass in how to sell anything to anyone*. Financial Times Prentice Hall.

Levinson, J. C. (2007) *Guerrilla Marketing: Easy and inexpensive strategies for making big profits from your small business* (4th edn). Houghton Mifflin.

Lund, P. (1995) *Building the Happiness-Centred Business* (2nd edn). Solutions Press.

Lund, P. (1998) *The Absolutely Critical Non-essentials*. Solutions Press.

Marshall, P. and Todd, B. (2010) *Ultimate Guide to Google Adwords: How to access 100 million people in 10 minutes* (2nd edn). Entrepreneur Press.

Reichheld, F. F. (2001) *The Loyalty Effect: The hidden force behind growth, profits and lasting value*. Harvard Business School Press.

Richer, J. (2009) *The Richer Way* (5th edn). Richer Publishing.

Rohm, R. A. (2006) *Positive Personality Profiles: Discover personality insights to understand yourself and others!* (4th edn). Personality Insights.

Stewart, G. (1999) *Successful Sales Management: How to make your team the best* (2nd edn). Financial Times Prentice Hall.

Townsend, Heather (2011) *FT Guide to Business Networking: How to use the power of online and offline networking for business success*. Financial Times Prentice Hall.

Tracy, B. (2008) *Eat That Frog! 21 great ways to stop procrastinating and get more done in less time* (2nd edn). Berrett-Koehlen.

Wilkinghoff, S. (2009) *Found Money: Simple strategies for uncovering the hidden profit and cash flow in your business*. John Wiley & Sons.

Index

Read On

9780273761990

9780273759539

9780273757986

Available to buy online and from all good bookshops
www.pearson-books.com